TOGETHER IN PRAYER

"The Liturgy of the Hours is the voice of the Church, that is, of the whole Mystical Body of Christ who joins the entire human community to himself. It is the very prayer that Christ himself, together with his Body, addresses to the Father."
(*Constitution on the Liturgy*, Chapter IV)

TOGETHER IN PRAYER

Learning To Love
the Liturgy of the Hours

"By your gift I will utter praise in the vast
assembly."(Psalm 22:26)

CHARLES E. MILLER, C.M.

ALBA·HOUSE   NEW·YORK

SOCIETY OF ST. PAUL, 2187 VICTORY BLVD., STATEN ISLAND, NEW YORK 10314

Library of Congress Cataloging-in-Publication Data

Miller, Charles Edward, 1929-
   Together in prayer: learning to love the Liturgy of the hours /
Charles E. Miller.
      p.   cm.
   Includes bibliographical references.
   ISBN 0-8189-0712-6
   1. Catholic Church. Liturgy of the hours. 2. Divine office.
I. Title.
BX2000.M55   1994
264'.0201 — dc20   94-23025
                                                          CIP

Nihil Obstat:
Rev. Msgr. Joseph Pollard, STD
Censor Deputatus

Imprimi Potest:
Jerome R. Herff, C.M.
Provincial, Province of the West

Imprimatur:
✠ Cardinal Roger Mahony
Archbishop of Los Angeles
May 10, 1994

The Nihil Obstat and Imprimatur are official declarations
that a book or pamphlet is free of doctrinal or moral
error. No implication is contained therein that those
who have granted the Nihil Obstat and Imprimatur agree
with the contents, opinions or statements expressed.

Produced and designed in the United States of America by the
Fathers and Brothers of the Society of St. Paul,
2187 Victory Boulevard, Staten Island, New York 10314,
as part of their communications apostolate.

ISBN: 0-8189-0712-6

Printing Information:

Current Printing - first digit   1   2   3   4   5   6   7   8   9   10

Year of Current Printing - first year shown

| 1994 | 1995 | 1996 | 1997 | 1998 | 1999 |

BOOKS BY CHARLES E. MILLER, C.M.

To Sow the Seed*
A Sense of Celebration
Making Holy the Day
Communicating Christ**
Repentance and Renewal***
Announcing the Good News**
Breaking the Bread**
Until He Comes***
Living in Christ
Love in the Language of Penance
Opening the Treasures
The Word Made Flesh**
As Rain That Falls
Mother and Disciple
Ordained to Preach

* with Oscar J. Miller, C.M.
** with Oscar J. Miller and Michael M. Roebert
***with John A. Grindel

All titles, with the exception of the first three,
have been published by Alba House.

"The Tradition of the Church proposes to the faithful certain rhythms of praying intended to nourish continual prayer."
Catechism of the Catholic Church, no. 2698

Contents

Part II
The Hours

Part III
More Psalms, The Canticles of Evening
and Morning Prayer, and Directives

"Give me people of prayer.
They will be able to do all things."
St. Vincent de Paul

Foreword

IN MANY PLACES THROUGHOUT THE WORLD groups of Christians gather to pray the Liturgy of the Hours together. Frequently they pray the Morning Prayer of the Church before daily Mass or, at the close of the workday, Evening Prayer. At times, individuals pause to celebrate these hours alone, in their own homes, or with their families. Priests and religious, in the spirit of their vocation, daily raise their hearts and voices to God in psalms of praise and thanksgiving. *Together in Prayer* is designed to help all of these people pray and celebrate the Church's daily liturgy with greater understanding and deeper love. It will, I hope, also attract others, who do not yet have the experience of praying the hours, to enter into this form of Divine Worship.

I am delighted that Father Charles E. Miller should offer us this work for he has been teaching courses and workshops on liturgy for many years. He also brings more than a scholarly approach to his subject. As a priest and a member of our Congregation, he has been actively participating in this form of community prayer for the greater part of his life. Through both his teaching and his lived experience, he has developed a rich knowledge of and a deep appreciation for the Liturgy of the Hours.

Because he wishes to share this treasure with everyone, he writes in a very simple, readable style, generously seasoned with good humor. He explains the composition of the hours themselves and gives suggestions for better understanding how to pray the various psalms and canticles. In so doing, he makes these centuries-old prayers very relevant for today.

Let me thank Father Miller for his labors in preparing this text. I trust that those who read it will find that it serves to deepen their prayer life and encourages them to join with others in praising God. This would indeed fulfill the purpose for which *Together in Prayer* was written.

Robert P. Maloney, C.M.
Superior General, Congregation of the Mission
Rome, April 22, 1994

The Liver and Onions of Prayer

*"At every opportunity pray in the Spirit,
using prayers and petitions of every sort." (Ephesians 6:18)*

ONE OF THE PLEASURES OF DINING OUT is that you can order from the menu. In a restaurant you do not have to eat what others eat, especially something you do not like. I have never, nor will I ever, order liver and onions in a restaurant. That surely is someone else's meat and my poison.

The Church is not like a restaurant, even though we rightly expect to be nourished there by the liturgy. We are not given a menu to select what we prefer, but we can be absolutely certain that in Word and Sacrament we are served a solid, varied, and healthful food which we can find nowhere else. The Vatican Council reminds us that "the Church, from the table of both the Word of God and of the Body of Christ, unceasingly offers to the faithful the bread of life in the sacred liturgy."[1]

Sometimes we may wish we did have a menu for Mass in order to avoid aspects which we find unpalatable. Among many items, I hear complaints about the music, the homily, the sign of peace, posture, and translations.

Can we please for a moment leave aside these and other

---

[1] *Constitution on Divine Revelation*, no. 21.

problems to consider one which is deeper? It is the problem of individualism. This outlook is so much a part of American culture that it affects how we pray, even without our suspecting it. Individualism is like the smog in the air we breathe. We cannot avoid it; we can only hope to overcome it.

This individualism makes it difficult for us to appreciate in a practical way that we form one body, one spirit in Christ, and that we have a responsibility for each other. Sometimes prayer which we are asked to offer and which is outgoing, unselfish and intended for the good of others is not satisfying. That is one reason why we may prefer to have a menu from which we could choose our private devotions rather than the liturgy, even though the Church teaches us that "every liturgical celebration is a sacred action which surpasses all others."[2]

All of this is leading to an observation about a form of liturgical prayer which is not in universal favor among Catholics, even though it should be. I am referring to the Liturgy of the Hours, the Divine Office, which is intended to be the prayer book of everyone in the Church. It is meant not just for priests, not just for religious, but for everyone.[3]

Unfortunately the format of the book is complicated, and even the version in a single volume is expensive (around twenty-five dollars). Those obstacles can be overcome. The real problem is that this prayer book does not have the purpose of satisfying individual needs or personal preference. It is by its nature an outgoing, unselfish kind of prayer.

At the heart of the Liturgy of the Hours, the Divine Office, is the praying of the psalms, those one hundred and fifty prayers which we have inherited from our ancestors in faith and which are the composition of the Holy Spirit. Consideration must be given first to the psalms. From their meaning and spirit we can enter into the meaning and spirit of the rest of the Liturgy of the Hours.

---

[2] *Constitution on the Sacred Liturgy*, no. 7.

[3] See the *General Instruction* of the *Liturgy of the Hours*, no. 27 and no. 32, as well as the *Constitution on the Sacred Liturgy*, no. 100.

It would be helpful to have some experience of the Liturgy of the Hours before reading what follows because this is not a "how-to" manual, even though I have included something on praying in community. It does not substitute for the General Instruction, the official document which is found in the front of the prayer book.

Sometimes I feel that the Liturgy of the Hours is like a treasure hidden in a field. I pray that this little book will help to uncover it. My hope is that by discovering this gift of God we will be eager to come together in prayer to proclaim his praises. Liturgy is not for some elite class in the Church. Liturgy is for people, and so is this book. I have tried to make it clear, simple, and succinct.

No one needs to like liver, but we should want to grow into loving the Liturgy of the Hours, this wonderful prayer book of the Church, which will expand our appreciation of all liturgy by forming within us an ecclesial, a "Church," spirituality.

Part I
GENERAL REFLECTIONS

"Christ joins all of humanity to himself, associating it with his own singing of this canticle of divine praise."

(Constitution on the Liturgy, no. 83)

"Pray with perseverance, be attentive to prayer, and pray in a spirit of thanksgiving."
(Colossians 4:1)

CHAPTER ONE

Praying the Church's Way

"We do not know how to pray as we ought." *(Romans 8:26)*

I HAVE BEEN PRAYING FOR AS LONG as I can remember. My earliest recollections, and I am not sure how far back they go, include images of praying at home even before the time I was old enough to go to church. My parents were good, devout Catholics, and they taught me to pray, not so much by instruction, as by example.

In the midst of the terrible depression of the 1930's, despite the expense, my parents sent me to St. Joseph's School in New Orleans, rather than to a public school. There I was taught by the Daughters of Charity. From them I learned new prayers, especially when it was time to prepare for my First Holy Communion. I do not recall any special fervor about the Mass until it was possible in the sixth grade for me to become an altar server. Something happened then to begin within me a love for the Eucharist. Not only did I look forward to going to Mass; I always wanted to serve, even when it was not my turn. Prayer began to mean the Mass. Even though I took pride in being able to recite the Latin responses flawlessly, I had little or no idea of what I was saying. I think it was the atmosphere of the rite more than its meaning which had an influence on me.

A big step came when at the tender age of thirteen I got on a train and travelled from my home in New Orleans to St. Vincent's College in Cape Girardeau, Missouri. This "college" was actually the Vincentian high school seminary. It was lovingly known by everyone associated with it simply as "Cape." From admirably dedicated Vincentian priests, I not only began to learn Latin and to discover the meaning of the prayers of the Mass, but I was also immersed in many forms of prayer according to the practice of the seminary.

Moving on to the Vincentian novitiate in Perryville, Missouri I was instructed in meditation and mental prayer, a revelation which helped me to develop a spirit of recollection and reflection.

After two years of novitiate, I had to struggle through three years of philosophy until I reached what seemed to me to be the big time, the major leagues, the bright lights of theology and Sacred Scripture which were taught by devoted Vincentians whom I will never forget. One of my great joys was to discover the writings of two great men. The first was Abbot Columba Marmion, the Irish parish priest turned Belgian Benedictine monk. He was responsible more than any other author or teacher for deepening my love affair with liturgical prayer. I practically memorized his books, *Christ the Life of the Soul* and *Christ in His Mysteries*. The second great man was Eugenio Pacelli, who became Pope Pius XII in 1939 (when I was but nine years old) and who died in 1958 (two years after I was ordained). My copies of his encyclicals, *Mystici Corporis Christi* (published in 1943) and *Mediator Dei* (1947), became so worn that they fell apart.

One day while still a seminarian, I don't remember just when, I was reading the eighth chapter of Paul's letter to the Romans. I came across his blunt statement: "We do not know how to pray as we ought" (8:26). With all the background I had enjoyed to that moment, I somewhat smugly thought that his words did not apply to me. I knew how to pray. Still I kept in mind his comment in the same verse: "The Holy Spirit helps us in our weakness."

In 1954 as I approached ordination as a subdeacon (in those days the obligation to pray the breviary began with subdiaconate, not with diaconate), I had a course in the psalms from Father Dan Martin, C.M. The class was wonderful, even though we had to spend a lot of time translating the psalms from Latin into English. By means of our study

I began to realize that the psalms are a different way to pray. I also recognized that, since they were inspired as was the rest of Scripture, they were a very specific means by which "the Holy Spirit helps us in our weakness."

Poetry Says It Right

The Holy Spirit has given us the psalms in the form of poetry, Hebrew poetry to be sure, but with the elements which make all good poetry a part of people's thought and speech. All of us do not have poetic ability, to say something memorable succinctly with imagination and beauty. If everyone were a poet, Shakespeare would not be immortal. His way of saying things has become so much a part of our language that a person who saw *Hamlet* for the first time complained that the play was nothing more than a tissue of cliches which she had heard all her life. Everyone is aware that "To be or not to be" is the question, whether they know that the line was written by Shakespeare or not.

I suppose that most of us have some favorite poems and remember at least a few lines from them. Tucked away in my memory is the wisdom of Alexander Pope who wrote, "Be not the first by whom the new is tried / Nor yet the last to lay the old aside," as well as his familiar "Fools rush in where angels fear to tread" and "A little learning is a dangerous thing."[1] I feel an awakening of conscience when I remember a scene in T.S. Eliot's play, *Murder in the Cathedral*, in which Archbishop Thomas Becket is tempted to seek martyrdom for his own glory. Eliot has the Archbishop say, "The last temptation is the greatest treason, / To do the right thing for the wrong reason."

Because poetry can develop a life of its own beyond the immediate intention of the author, we give a personal interpretation to its meaning. Robert Frost in his poem, "Birches," wrote "Earth's the right place for love. I don't know where it's likely to go better." I think

---

[1] From *An Essay on Criticism*.

of the incarnation, which Frost did not, and I am grateful that God so loved the world that he created it to be the right place for his Son.

At a time when people were more literate in poetry than they are now, lovers turned to poems when they found it difficult to express their feelings in their own words. Young people used to know that Elizabeth Barrett Browning (who died in 1861) wrote one of the most eloquent love poems in the English language. They were delighted to make her words their own:

> "How do I love thee? Let me count the ways.
> I love thee to the depth and breadth and height
> My soul can reach, when feeling out of sight
> For the ends of Being and ideal Grace."

Now we rely on Hallmark cards when we think that their words are the very best and ours are not.

Individualism and Piety

Even though the psalms are great poetry, not a few people prefer to use their own words in prayer. Of course there is a special value in sentiments which spring almost spontaneously from the human heart, however awkwardly they may be expressed. Liturgical documents insist that there is not only room for individual prayer, there is a necessity for it.[2] Perhaps, however, secular individualism influences piety more than we suspect[3] so that prayer in the first instance has come to mean a solitary experience rather than a corporate expression by a people God has made his own to praise his glory.[4] We should never deny that each of us individually is precious in the eyes of God, who as a Father delights

---

[2] See, for example, no. 13 in the *Constitution on the Sacred Liturgy*.

[3] This problem has been ably treated in *Habits of the Heart: Individualism and Commitment in American Life* by Robert N. Bellah and associates.

[4] See Ephesians 1:14.

in even the most halting attempts at prayer by any child of his, but we may need to keep in mind the caution of St. Paul: "We do not know how to pray as we ought."

After all, God is transcendent, far above us and beyond the pale of direct experience. In prayer we are feeling out of sight for the ends of Being and ideal Grace. We should not rush in where angels fear to tread. Can we learn more about prayer? We had better, since a little learning is a dangerous thing. If we need to put aside old ways of praying, we must not be the last to do so. If we embrace the psalms, we will not be the first by whom these great prayers have been tried. For more than three thousand years they have helped devout people, Jewish and Christian, to count the ways in which we are to love God and that he loves us. Be assured that the psalms are the right way to pray and that there is no place where prayers are likely to go better than in the pages of Sacred Scripture. To pray or not to pray is not the question. The question is whether we wish to take the effort to learn and to offer the prayers which the Holy Spirit has inspired and which the Church presents to us in the Liturgy of the Hours.

The Church's Prayer Book

Following the Vatican Council, a word came into prominence in the vocabulary of Catholics. That word is liturgy. I think most Catholics recognize at least in a general way that liturgy is the official community prayer of the Church, but the tendency has been to limit its meaning to the celebration of the Eucharist ("What time is liturgy?" people ask, meaning "What time is Mass?"). Actually liturgy includes all seven sacraments, the liturgical year, and that book which used to be called the breviary or the Divine Office and which is now properly termed the Liturgy of the Hours.

Applicable to the Liturgy of the Hours is this declaration of the Council: "Every liturgical celebration, because it is an action of Christ the priest and of his body the Church, is a sacred action surpassing all others. No other action of the Church can match its claim to efficacy nor equal the degree of it."[5]

The Liturgy of the Hours has been formed and shaped by the great central idea of the Second Vatican Council which declares that "it has pleased God to save us and to make us holy, not merely as individuals without any mutual bonds, but by forming us into a single people, a people who worship him in truth and who serve him in holiness."[6] It draws its main content and its themes from the psalms. The corporate prayer of Israel has become the corporate prayer of the Church.

The Liturgy of the Hours also includes canticles. These are lyrical prayers from different parts of the Bible, both Old and New Testaments, which were not incorporated into the book of Psalms, but like the psalms they are prayers which were inspired by the Holy Spirit. The Church has added other prayers, especially the orations and the intercessions, which in our current edition of the Liturgy of the Hours have been culled, for the most part, from manuscripts of prayer books in the Vatican library which go back through the centuries.

Liturgical prayer is always a dialogue; not only do we speak to God, but God speaks to us. And so the Liturgy of the Hours always includes readings from Sacred Scripture. Most people have favorite passages from Scripture, and it is good to return to them again and again. And yet the Church wishes us to grow in our knowledge and love of all of God's Word. The Second Vatican Council was explicit: "The treasures of the Bible are to be opened more lavishly, so that richer fare may be provided for the faithful at the table of God's Word."[7] The readings found throughout the Liturgy of the Hours help to achieve this wish of the Church. These readings have been arranged in such a way that together with those presented in the lectionary for Mass we cover virtually the entire content of the Bible.

---

[5] Constitution on the Sacred Liturgy, no. 7.

[6] See the Dogmatic Constitution on the Church, no. 9, the Constitution on the Church in the Modern World, no. 32, and the Decree on the Church's Missionary Activity, no. 2. This statement is found verbatim in all three documents.

[7] Constitution on the Sacred Liturgy, no. 51.

Liturgy Is Real Prayer

We will have made progress in ecclesial spirituality, a spirituality which is specifically Catholic, when prayer in the first instance means liturgical prayer, prayer together through Christ, and not a solitary experience. Recently while visiting a seminary (postman's holiday), I was chatting with the spiritual director. He asked me what I taught in our seminary. I replied, in what I intended to be a jocular manner, that I taught the only two subjects a priest really needs, homiletics and liturgy. The mood changed immediately. He said in very measured words, "I would hope that they would also be men of prayer." I responded, too strongly I am afraid, "What do you mean? Isn't liturgy the prayer of the Church?" Then I laughed to lighten the mood and so did he. And yet the conversation reminded me that we still need to embrace the truth that the liturgy is prayer, real prayer, and indeed the highest form of prayer.

Sometimes I wish that someone in the Church had the power to move people to love this prayer book of the Church as readily as a person can move a document from one file to another in a computer. I am convinced, however, that with faith we can see how beautiful this compilation called the Liturgy of the Hours really is. It graciously invites us to come before the Lord together in prayer. No other form of prayer can adequately substitute for it.

Effort is needed to master the Church's prayer. The great musician, Pablo Casals, continued to practice four or five hours a day when he was over eighty years old. Someone asked him why he still worked so hard. He responded, "Because I have a notion that I am making some progress."

Progress in praying the Liturgy of the Hours requires effort, but every effort is worthwhile because in offering this prayer of the Church we are doing the right thing, and by absorbing its spirit we are praying for the right reason. God cares enough about us that through the Church he has given us the very best in the Liturgy of the Hours.

"Together they devoted themselves to constant prayer."
(Acts 1:14)

CHAPTER TWO

Knowing the Psalms

"The Spirit helps us in our weakness." (Romans 8:26)

THE PSALMS, SOMEWHAT LIKE JESUS, are both divine and human. They are divine in that they were inspired by the Holy Spirit as was the rest of the Bible. They are human in that they developed over a period of some seven hundred years from the sentiments of God's people who cried out to him in faith according to their cultural, historical, and theological backgrounds. Some psalms were composed before the exile in 587 B.C. and others after. Scholars judge that elements of these prayers are very old, going back indefinitely into Israelite history. We embrace the psalms as the right way to pray because their author is the Holy Spirit, but at times we find the psalms difficult because the Holy Spirit worked through a human community of men and women who are far removed from us not only by centuries but by social, cultural, and sometimes theological differences.

Pope Pius XII emphasized that basic to arriving at the intention of the divine author of the Scriptures is the effort to discover the intention of the human authors of the Scriptures.[1] We should not, therefore, be disappointed if some psalms do not at first appeal to us or do not seem to agree with our spirituality. The study of the psalms

---

[1] This is the central idea of his encyclical, *Divino Afflante Spiritu*, published in 1943.

can be a life-long endeavor, but on the other hand so much available scholarship has already gone into the psalms that with relative ease we can learn what is basic for understanding them. Excellent commentaries abound for those who wish to pursue the exegesis of the psalms in depth, but here I present only those simple, clear ideas which are essential to praying the psalms intelligently and devoutly as the Church intends us to pray them in the Liturgy of the Hours.

Classification of Psalms

There are several approaches to classifying the psalms, only two of which we will look at here. The first is to consider the psalms according to literary types.[2] In English and most contemporary languages, poems can be classified as lyrics, dramas, narratives, or epics. Psalms can be classified according to literary types as (1) Psalms of Thanksgiving and Praise; (2) Psalms of Lament or Petition; and (3) Psalms of Trust. Secondly, classifications may be made according to the subject matter of the psalms, so that some scholars identify royal psalms, wisdom psalms, and salvation history psalms. Such classifications are not exhaustive and one psalm may overlap two or more categories.

The advantage of determining the type of psalm is that you feel at home with the prayer and can enter readily into its meaning and spirit. Even if you do not think of yourself as a Scripture scholar, you will be delightfully surprised at how easy it usually is to recognize the type.

Thanksgiving and Praise

When the priest introduces the Eucharistic Prayer at Mass, he exhorts us to enter into its meaning with these words: "Let us give thanks to the Lord our God." We respond, "It is right to give him thanks

---

[2] Much credit is given to the German scholar, Hermann Gunkel (1862-1932).

and praise." Joining together these two words of our response, thanks and praise, is helpful not only at Mass but when considering the psalms. The fact is that in Hebrew there is no word for thanksgiving. The Hebrew word which is usually translated as thanksgiving sounds like "toda." In the psalms it means "praise" in the sense of acknowledging or expressing some admirable quality about God which has redounded to the benefit of his people. Thanksgiving psalms are offered to God in response to his marvelous qualities and especially his saving actions. They usually begin with an expression of thanks and then proclaim how God has favored the psalmist in time of need. They are often composed in the first person singular, but they do not exclude the community from participating. An example is psalm 138 which begins, "I thank you, Lord, with all my heart; you have heard the words of my mouth." This psalm is found at Evening Prayer on Tuesday of Week IV.

Psalms of praise have a somewhat set structure. They begin with an invitation to praise the Lord, for example, "Sing a new song to the Lord, his praise in the assembly of the faithful" or "Ring out your joy to the Lord, O you just, for praise is fitting for loyal hearts." The body of the psalm presents the reason for praise, for example, "For the Lord takes delight in his people. He crowns the poor with salvation," or "For the word of the Lord is faithful and all his works to be trusted. The Lord loves justice and right and fills the earth with his love." There is no formal conclusion, although the invitation which began the psalm is sometimes repeated or a petition is expressed, such as, "May your love be upon us, O Lord, as we place all our hope in you." Some authors separate psalms of praise from those of thanksgiving, but for the purposes of the Liturgy of the Hours there is no need to make this distinction.

Examples of the psalms of thanksgiving and praise can be found in Morning Prayer for any day. Morning Prayer consists of a first psalm, an Old Testament canticle, and a second psalm. The second psalm in every instance is a psalm of thanksgiving or praise. A little over one-fourth of all the psalms are of this type. Although they are not the most numerous, they are the heart of the Psalter and from them flows a life which influences the other psalms. In fact, the Jews used the generic term *tehillim*, which means "praises" to refer to all the psalms. (The word "psalm" is from a Greek word which means a stringed instrument, as suggested by the type of instrument which would often accompany the singing of the prayers.) Psalms of praise set the tone of the Liturgy of the Hours. Further consideration will be given to them in the chapter on Morning Prayer.

Psalms of Lament or Petition

Psalms of lament or petition emerged from human sufferings caused by distress over a wretched predicament, by affliction due to injustice, by physical or verbal attacks by enemies or treachery by friends, by sickness and the fear of death, or by the consequences of sin. They begin with a plea to the Lord, or even an unabashed demand for his attention. Within the body of the psalm there is a vivid description of the cause of distress, then a petition for help which at times asks the Lord to punish or rebuke the wicked, and then an expression of hope. Sometimes the conclusion contains words of assurance expressed by a priest. The structure is not rigid; the elements follow no specific order and are sometimes repeated. Laments are both individual and collective, but again individual prayers never exclude the community. This type accounts for about sixty psalms.

Psalm 5 which is found in Morning Prayer for Monday of Week I, is an example of an individual lament. It begins with a plea to the Lord:

> To my words give ear, O Lord,
> give heed to my groaning.
> Attend to the sound of my cries,
> my King and my God.

Distress is caused by enemies who are described as follows:

> No truth can be found in their mouths,
> their heart is all mischief,

> their throat a wide-open grave,
> all honey their speech.

The psalmist has trust in the Lord and says to him:

> All those you protect shall be glad
> and ring out their joy.
> You shelter them, in you they rejoice,
> those who love your name.

The psalm ends on a note of hope and confidence:

> It is you who bless the just man, Lord:
> you surround him with favor as with a shield.

Psalms of Trust

It is possible to combine psalms of trust with those of lament as a single type. I judge that they are worth a separate classification, even though there are only about nine such psalms. They are more positive in tone than the psalms of lament and describe more vividly the wonderful saving works of God on behalf of his people. A favorite of many people is psalm 16 which is found in Night Prayer for Thursdays. A few verses manifest its qualities:

> Preserve me, God, I take refuge in you.
> I say to the Lord: "You are my God.
> My happiness lies in you alone.
> O Lord, it is you who are my portion and cup;
> it is you yourself who are my prize.
> The lot marked out for me is my delight;
> welcome indeed the heritage that falls to me.
> You will show me the path of life,
> the fullness of joy in your presence,
> at your right hand happiness for ever."

Royal Psalms, Wisdom Psalms, and Salvation History Psalms

Royal psalms flow from experiences in the life of a king of Israel. (Psalms which refer directly to God as King are not royal psalms; usually they are psalms of thanksgiving and praise.) The human king was looked upon as a representative of God, as a viceroy who ruled not in his own name but in the name of the Lord, and who therefore was a religious figure. At times he performed the functions of a priest. These ancient psalms are prayed in the Church as understood in the light of further and full revelation which brings the figure of Christ the King into a sharp focus.[3] The Liturgy of the Hours applies them, therefore, to Christ the King. Good examples are psalm 2 from the Office of Readings on Sunday of Week I and psalm 110 from Sunday Evening Prayer.

Wisdom psalms are meditations or reflections in the presence of God on the meaning of life and its problems. The very first psalm belongs to this type (see Office of Readings for Sunday of Week I) and sets one of the major themes of the Psalter: the good man standing against evil.

Salvation history psalms are poetic summaries of God's saving actions in the tradition of his people. (The Fourth Eucharistic Prayer shares in the style and spirit of these psalms.) An example is psalm 105 which is prayed in the Office of Readings during Advent and Lent on Saturdays of Week I.

Direction or Orientation of the Psalms

The psalms are manifestly God-centered. In fact, one hundred and thirty-three of them mention God in the very first verse, but they do not all speak to God directly. In our contemporary Christian spirituality we almost always offer our prayers immediately and

---

[3] See no. 55 in the *Dogmatic Constitution on the Church* in which this principle is invoked when treating of Mary in the Old Testament.

personally to God. We are comfortable with praying as Jesus taught us and we address God directly and simply as "Our Father." In contrast the psalms are almost like the man who jumped on his horse and "ran off in all directions." Psalm 1 is a wisdom psalm which is not addressed to God but which is the voicing of a reflection before the community gathered in prayer: "Happy indeed is the man who follows not the counsel of the wicked." Psalm 2, a royal psalm, addresses the rulers of the earth and admonishes them "to serve the Lord with awe." Psalm 3 is in the familiar mode which we usually follow: "Arise, Lord; save me, my God." The same can be said of psalms 4 through 8. Some psalms are an exhortation to the community: "Ring out your joy to the Lord, O you just; for praise is fitting for loyal hearts" (psalm 33). In a few psalms we hear the voice of God. An example is psalm 91 wherein God says of the person who trusts in him:

> Since he clings to me in love, I will free him;
> I will protect him for he knows my name.
> When he calls I shall answer: "I am with you."
> I will save him in distress and give him glory

All the psalms, whatever their type, have in common a deep faith in the presence and involvement of God in the lives of his people. Prayer, therefore, is not necessarily directed to God but it is always offered in his never failing and always providential presence. A simple, eloquent expression of this faith, spoken directly to God, is found in the thirty-five verses of psalm 104, only a few of which I quote here:

> From your dwelling you water the hills;
> earth drinks its fill of your gifts.
> You make the grass grow for the cattle
> and the plants to serve man's needs,
> that he may bring forth bread from the earth
> and wine to cheer man's heart;
> oil to make him glad
> and bread to strengthen man's heart.

A Few Theological Points

The psalms in varied ways are all God-centered. In union with the people of the covenant which God made with Abraham, we cry out "Lord." In union with Christ who shed his blood in the new and everlasting covenant, we cry out "Father." But there are not two Gods. The God and Lord of Abraham, Isaac, and Jacob is the God and Father of Jesus Christ. The God of Israel is the God of Christians.[4]

We do, however, live in the light of fuller revelation, not only because we are of the Christian era, but because we are the recipients of the corporate wisdom of the Church which has pondered God's revelation for almost twenty centuries. If we find an expression in the psalms which we consider theologically unsophisticated or even offensive to our Christian sensibilities, we are not contrasting truth with falsehood. We have encountered simple directness as opposed to a nuanced refinement.

Is it polite to thrust at God the demand of psalm 13?

> How long, O Lord, will you forget me?
> How long will you hide your face?
> Look at me, answer me, Lord my God!

The psalmist would answer by saying, "Of course it is. Is there anyone else I can turn to? The Lord is the only one who can help me and at the moment he seems far off."

We believe that there is a distinction between the sin and the sinner, and we try to hate the sin while loving the sinner. Hebrew thought made no such distinction. Reality was concrete. Since sin is wicked, sinners are wicked people. Upon whom can we depend if not on God when sinners oppress us? And when we turn to God we leave it to him to make all the distinctions necessary.

The author of psalm 94 is fired with indignation. He cries out:

---

[4] "Lord" is the usual and appropriate substitution for "Yahweh," since this sacred tetragrammaton according to tradition should never be pronounced aloud.

> O Lord, avenging God,
> avenging God, appear!
> Judge of the earth, arise,
> give the proud what they deserve.

The psalmist has good reason to be indignant, as he indicates:

> How long shall the wicked triumph?
> They crush your people, Lord,
> they afflict the ones you have chosen.
> They kill the widow and the stranger
> and murder the fatherless child.

He goes on to complain about those who are pledged to uphold the law but who blatantly violate it:

> Can judges who do evil be your friends?
> They do injustice under cover of law;
> they attack the life of the just
> and condemn innocent blood.

In the face of such evil, the psalmist has only one recourse, to place his trust in the Lord:

> As for me, the Lord will be a stronghold;
> my God will be the rock where I take refuge.

As we pray the psalms, we should be open to learning the ways of God. Some Christians fear the end times when God will come, they think, as the vengeful judge who will remember our every human foible, as well as our heinous sins, and he will allow no evil of ours to go unpunished. By contrast the psalmist sees himself as the plaintiff, not as the accused before God, and he is eager to appear in God's court because he believes that only through God's powerful judgment will justice come to an unjust world:

> The Lord sits enthroned forever.

He has set up his throne for judgment;
he will judge the world with justice,
he will judge the people with his truth.[5]

Prayer Leads to Action

During a liturgy meeting, a group of priests were saying Evening
Prayer together when the lights went out in the chapel. A Dominican
stood up and said, "My brothers, let us take this opportunity to reflect
on the philosophical essence of light and darkness." A Franciscan
stood and said, "My brothers, let us take this moment of darkness to
thank God for the beauty of our sister, the light." A Jesuit went and
changed the fuse. Contemplation and prayer lead to action. The
psalms will teach us to love the poor, to defend the downtrodden, to
assist the alien, to cherish the lowly, and to embrace all of God's people
in love.

St. Athanasius observed that "the psalms have a unique value in
that most of the Scriptures speaks *to* us, whereas the psalms speak *for*
us." In various and wondrous ways, especially through the psalms, the
Holy Spirit helps us in our weakness to pray as we ought.

---

[5] Psalm 9 in the Office of Readings, Week I.

CHAPTER THREE

The Poetry of the Psalms

"Sing a new song to the Lord." (Psalm 98)

T HE HOLY SPIRIT INSPIRED THE PRAYER of the psalms in the form of poetry. The poetic elements, although not essential to the meaning of the prayer, provide delight to some psalms, vividness to others, and memorable expressions to them all.

A woman at a cocktail party was trying to impress James Thurber, the humorist, by telling him how much she had enjoyed reading one of his books in a French translation. Thurber responded by saying, "I know what you mean. My works lose something in the original."

The psalms are Hebrew poetry. In contrast to Thurber's ironic remark, the psalms lose something in the translation, and yet scholars in converting the ancient Hebrew of the psalms into contemporary languages have succeeded in preserving at least two poetic elements: structure and imagery.

Structure of the Psalms

The structure of Hebrew poetry is based on parallelism. Two, and sometimes three, verses stand in relationship to each other. Examples are found in psalm 86 which is prayed at Monday Night Prayer. Three forms are the most common.

The first form is based on restatement, which some scholars call synonymous parallelism. The same thing is said in two ways:

> Preserve my life, for I am faithful;
> save the servant who trusts in you.

In the second form, which is termed complementary, there is a progression in the thought so that the second verse (sometimes a third verse) complements or completes the meaning of the first:

> Turn your ear, O Lord, and give answer
> for I am poor and needy.

The third form, which is less common than the first two, expresses contrast and is sometimes termed antithetic parallelism as in psalm 20:

> Some trust in chariots or horses,
> but we in the name of the Lord.

A triplet may combine two forms of parallelism:

> Show me, Lord, your way
> so that I may walk in your truth.
> Guide my heart to fear your name.

In this example the first and third verses are synonymous, but the first and second are complementary. Try reading aloud the following excerpts from psalm 86 so that you may get the feel of the rhythm which parallelism creates. Pause slightly at the end of each line:

> Give joy to your servant, O Lord,
> for to you I lift up my soul.

> O Lord, you are good and forgiving,
> full of love to all who call.

> In the day of distress I will call
> and surely you will reply.

> The proud have risen against me;
> ruthless men seek my life:
> to you they pay no heed.

> But you, God of mercy and compassion,
> abounding in love and truth,
> turn and take pity on me.

Examples of parallelism are found in Jesus' Sermon on the Mount:

> Ask and you will receive.
> Seek and you will find.
> Knock and it will be opened for you.[1]

The rhythm of parallelism is so appealing that it is not lacking in English poetry. Alexander Pope seems to have an endless supply of couplets which reflect Hebrew parallelism. His couplets are iambic pentameter, which Shakespeare employed before him, and they rhyme:

> Hope springs eternal in the human breast;
> Man never is, but always to be blessed.[2]

William Wordsworth composed a very clever sonnet on the experience of writing within the limits which the sonnet form imposes. He begins the poem with a synonymous triplet:

> Nuns fret not at their convent's narrow room;
> And hermits are contented with their cells;
> And students with their narrow citadels.

Then because of the rhyme scheme which the sonnet requires, he finds that he cannot continue the parallels, and yet his theme is that he finds delight in the challenge which the restrictions of the literary

---

[1] Matthew 7:7.
[2] From *An Essay on Man*.

form impose. Later Robert Frost was to say of free verse, which requires neither a set meter nor a rhyme scheme, that it is like playing tennis with the net down.

The psalmists played tennis in the proper manner, but translations cannot reproduce their techniques in every regard, especially the meter, the pattern of accented syllables which give poetry a rhythmic beat. The translation into English known as the Grail Psalter has arranged the words so that in each verse there are two or three strong accents but without a strict pattern. Read aloud the following verses in which the accents are marked:

> Oh Lórd, you are góod and forgíving,
> full of lóve to áll who cáll.
> Give héed, O Lórd, to my práyer,
> and atténd to the sóund of my vóice.[3]

When praying aloud it is not necessary to be conscious of hitting the accents. When you take your time and pronounce the syllables distinctly, the accents will occur naturally.

There is a tension between creating a translation which is poetic and suitable for praying aloud, especially by singing, and one which is scholarly and expressly faithful to the original text. A highly successful translation into an English poetic form is the following verse from psalm 29:

> The Lord's voice flashes flames of fire.

When you read that verse aloud you can almost see the lightning and hear the thunder. Less poetic but slightly more faithful to the original text is the following translation of the same verse:

> The voice of the Lord strikes fiery flames.

---

[3] The version of the Liturgy of the Hours which is published in London by Collins and in Dublin by Talbot supplies the accent marks for the psalms, but the versions published in the United States do not.

The Music of the Psalms

The poetry of the psalms is best expressed when they are sung. The words of the psalms are lyrics which were set to music. We have no record of what the melodies were. In fact, only rarely would any musical notations have been written. People readily memorized the musical accompaniment, not only because the melodies were simple but because their memories were facile.

Psalm 47 begins with a direction by the psalmist to the worshippers and then continues in such a jubilant spirit that we can readily imagine its being performed by an Afro-American choir of enthusiastic singers:

> All you people, clap your hands,
> cry to God with shouts of joy!
> The Lord goes up with trumpet blast.
> Sing praise to God, sing praise.
> Sing praise to our king, sing praise.

Even if the ideal of singing the psalms is not achieved with any frequency, the musical and poetic elements can at least be moderately experienced when those praying pause at the end of each line and pronounce the words deliberately and distinctly.

Acrostic Psalms

The structure of some psalms is determined by a pattern in which the initial letters of the verses, or groupings of verses, follow the sequence of the Hebrew alphabet. This technique is totally lost in translation. The result is that we may feel that acrostic psalms lack any apparent form of organization. A lengthy example of the acrostic style is psalm 37, which is prayed in the Office of Readings for Tuesday of Week II. Even if the technique were transferred to a translation, I suspect that its effect would still be lost on us. A simple attempt at this technique would look something like this:

> Almighty is the Lord, our God,
> Bringing joy to those who are faithful,
> Confirming their goodness with his gifts.
> Doubt not the Lord in time of trial.
> Even if he seems far away,
> Forget not his loving kindness.
> Great is the Lord our God.

Only eight psalms use the acrostic form of organization.

Imagery in the Psalms

Poetry comes alive through figurative language, through analogies and metaphors, and all those devices which may be included under the term imagery. Imagery appeals to the senses. It helps us to see, to hear, and to feel what would otherwise be abstract. By means of imagery poetry answers the question, "What is it like?" Carl Sandburg thought that fog was like a cat:

> The fog comes
> on little cat feet.
> It sits looking
> over harbor and city
> on silent haunches
> and then moves us.

Sandburg was satisfied that this image was enough to make his words true poetry. T.S. Eliot shows how the same image can be expanded more imaginatively:

> The yellow fog that rubs its back upon the window-panes,
> The yellow smoke that rubs its muzzle on the window-panes,
> Licked its tongue into the corners of the evening,
> Lingered upon the pools that stand in drains,
> Let fall upon its back the soot that falls from chimneys,

Slipped by the terrace, made a sudden leap.
And seeing that it was a soft October night,
Curled once around the house, and fell asleep.[4]

The effectiveness of imagery is that it engages the senses and not merely the mind. Imagery is one of the appealing, human elements of the psalms, but Hebrew poetry often adds its own dimension to imagery. That dimension is the feelings of the psalmist and those who pray the psalm. When the psalmist proclaims that the Lord is his rock, we may conclude that he means to say that the Lord is solid and dependable. But in psalm 18 when he says, "I love you, Lord, my rock," we do not conclude that he is comparing the Lord, *salva reverentia*, to his pet rock. Rather he has reflected on how a person who is pursued by violent enemies feels when he can take refuge behind a huge rock. He feels safe and secure, just as the psalmist feels safe and secure by taking refuge in the Lord. As elegant as is Eliot's image of the fog as a cat, my response is delightful admiration but not an identification with a feeling.

Some people find a passage in the Song of Songs to be almost ludicrous:

> Hark! my lover — here he comes
> springing across the mountains,
> leaping across the hills.
> My lover is like a gazelle
> or a young stag.

This analogy, which envisions the lover to be like a gazelle, cannot be understood as it would in English poetry. The point is that the beloved is in awe at the energetic grace of the gazelle, and that is how she feels when she thinks of her lover: she is full of awe. The comparison is not of the beloved with a gazelle, but of feeling with feeling.

---

[4] From his poem, "The Love Song of J. Alfred Prufrock."

Gerard Manley Hopkins, the Jesuit priest poet, sometimes adds the Hebrew mode to his imagery. He does so in his mystical poem, "The Windhover: To Christ our Lord." In unusual images he pictures the flight of a windhover, an English falcon. He marvels at the graceful power of the bird, and in his mind's eye he sees an ice skater cutting a figure which looks like a ribbon, tied in a bow:

> Then off, off on swing,
> As a skate's heel sweeps smooth on a bow-bend.
> The hurl and gliding rebuffed the big wind.

The metaphor seems inappropriate (how is Christ like a bird which in turn is like an ice skater?) until Father Hopkins refers explicitly to the Hebrew mode:

> My heart in hiding
> Stirred for a bird,
> the achieve of, the mastery of the thing!

The stirring which he feels in witnessing the falcon in its flight is like the stirring he feels when he thinks of Christ in his passion. And so when I proclaim that the Lord is my shepherd, I not only envision the tender guidance and nurturing of a keeper of fleecy animals, I also sense the serene security of the sheep and I believe that in God's providence I shall want for nothing.

A powerful image of God introduces the majestic psalm 104:

> Lord, God, how great you are,
> clothed in majesty and glory,
> wrapped in light as in a robe!
> You make the clouds your chariot,
> and walk on the wings of the wind.

The poetry is intended not primarily to describe God but to elicit from us the sentiment expressed in the first verse: "Lord, God, how great you are."

Understanding and appreciating Hebrew poetry helps us to offer the psalms in a devout manner according to the human dimension of these eloquent expressions of what it means to be a people who come together in prayer.

*"Present your need to God in every form
of prayer and in petitions full of gratitude."
(Philippians 4:6)*

CHAPTER FOUR

Apostolic Prayer

*"I ask that supplications, prayers, petitions, and
thanksgiving be offered for everyone. . . . This is good
and pleasing to God our Savior." (1 Timothy 2:1)*

THE PSALMS COVER ALMOST EVERY human sentiment: joy and
sorrow, pain and healing, thanksgiving and desperation,
praise and complaint. The unvarnished humanity of the
psalms is one reason they have endured through the centuries, but it
is also a reason why some people find them difficult, if not impossible,
to pray. We can readily pray psalms which fit our moods and our needs,
but what do we do when a psalm is totally different from how we are
thinking or feeling?

I have in mind psalm 88 which is assigned to Friday night prayer.
It is a psalm of lament and it is the bleakest of all one hundred and fifty
psalms. Taking a "cue" from the game of pool, we say of a person who
is in trouble that he is behind the eight ball. The author of psalm 88 is
behind two eight balls. The prayer begins as do many psalms:

> Lord my God, I call for help by day;
> I cry at night before you.
> Let my prayer come into your presence.
> O turn your ear to my cry.

But after a long list of human woes it concludes on a note, not of
optimism, but of desperation:

> Friend and neighbor you have taken away:
> my one companion is darkness.

That is the end of the psalm. It echoes the sentiment of Job who
during the worst part of his trial cried out:

> My days are swifter than a weaver's shuttle;
> they come to an end without hope.
> Remember that my life is like the wind;
> I shall not see happiness again.[1]

Like everyone, I have had my bad days but I have never felt as bad
as either the psalmist or Job: "My one companion is darkness. — I shall
never see happiness again." That's awful. I can hardly think of a bleaker
outlook, and yet it is a reality for some people, not only for the hungry
and the homeless, but for the abused wife, the abandoned husband, the
unloved child.

The liturgy calls us to pray this psalm not only for people who are
in desperate situations, but in their persons, to become their heart and
their voice before God. Some of these people turn to God in prayer,
if not in the words of psalm 88, at least in its sentiments. I want to unite
with them in their prayer. Some of these people may never think of
God. I want to pray in their stead.

Psalm 88 yields ready application to many forms of human
misery. I think of little children, hidden in their mother's womb, who
are threatened with abortion when I say:

> You have laid me in the depths of the tomb,
> in places that are dark, in the depths.
> You have taken away my friends
> and made me hateful in their sight.

---

[1] Job 7:6-7.

> Imprisoned, I cannot escape;
> my eyes are sunken with grief.

I envision young people who are caught up in gang violence, who can be murdered at any time in a foolish drive-by shooting or as part of a horrible form of initiation into the gang:

> Wretched, close to death from my youth,
> I have borne your trials, I am numb.

Drug addicts come to mind as I pray:

> My life is on the brink of the grave.
> I am reckoned as one in the tomb;
> I have reached the end of my strength.

Liturgical prayer does not exclude our personal, individual sentiments, but it does seek to raise us above and beyond our own limited world to be like Jesus who opened his arms on the cross to embrace everyone. The spirituality of liturgical prayer is found in an emphatic fashion in the Prayer of the Faithful (also known as the General Intercessions) in which we are asked to intercede "for all humanity." As a rule the intentions include prayers for the needs of the whole Church, for public authorities and the salvation of the world, for those oppressed by any need, and for the local community.[2] That is a generous, outgoing kind of prayer. It is centered on the needs of others, not my own. The psalms call us to yet another dimension, not only to pray for others, but to pray in their persons.

In the early 1970's I joined Father Philip Van Linden, C.M., who was then on the faculty of St. John's Seminary in California, in giving workshops on the Liturgy of the Hours. We coined the term, "apostolic prayer," in our teachings about the psalms. We recognized that the call to be an apostle meant going out to people in the name of Christ, and

---

[2] *General Instruction* of the *Roman Missal*, no. 45.

so we thought that "apostolic prayer" designated what we had in mind for the psalms. Apostolic praying means offering the psalms not only for people but in their very person. It involves us in the lives of others. It means becoming their heart and their voice before God.

Experience Leads to Apostolic Prayer

Through experience and reflection we can grow in our appreciation of the psalms and learn to pray them apostolically. Please allow me to relate some very personal experiences. In September of 1978 my mother became seriously ill because of old age and diabetes. I was blessed to be able to put her under the care of the Sister Servants of Mary in Mary Health of the Sick Hospital in Newbury Park, California. When I visited her, I would try to pray the rosary with her. That devotion had been an important part of her life, and yet I could get no response. I would put the beads in her hand and say, "Come on, Mom. Let's say the Hail Mary together." Nothing. She stared at the rosary as if she could not recognize this sacramental which had been precious to her all her life. It was very sad.

The Spirit helped me to pray in this situation. In Daytime Prayer on Monday of Week III, I found psalm 71. It is the prayer of a person who is seventy-one years of age or older:

> In you, O Lord, I take refuge;
> let me never be put to shame.
> Do not reject me now that I am old;
> when my strength fails do not forsake me.

In this prayer I became the heart and the voice of my mother who could no longer lift her heart and her voice in prayer. The hospital was filled with other ladies in conditions similar to my mother's. I wanted to pray in their persons too. Meanwhile my father, although seven years older than my mother, was in pretty good condition and his mind remained very sharp. He too loved the rosary, and now he prayed it almost constantly since his eyesight was so poor that reading or even watching television was very difficult. I wanted to support him in his prayerful spirit and to be also his voice when I prayed in psalm 71:

> O God, you have taught me from my youth
> and I proclaim your wonders still.
> Now that I am old and grey-headed,
> do not forsake me, God.

My mother died in October of 1980 at the age of eighty-eight and my father died the following July at the age of ninety-five, but I will always be grateful that through them I learned to pray psalm 71 apostolically. Back in 1978 when I first put my mother in the hospital, I was only forty-eight years old. As of this writing I am sixty-four and I am old and grey-headed as was the psalmist. I can pray psalm 71 in my own name, as well as in the person of the elderly, but I hope there are very many devout people, both old and young, who are offering this psalm as an apostolic prayer in union with me.

The Concept of Solidarity

Apostolic prayer draws its spirit from the Old Testament concept of solidarity. Devout Israelites had an intense realization of their unity as the people of God. Consequently, when a psalm is designated as an "individual lament," the label refers more to grammatical construction than to a single person who exclusively offers the prayer. In the psalms the community speaks in the first person singular by identifying with a representative, usually a priest or a king. (Because of the principle of solidarity, the suffering servant in Isaiah can be understood to be the whole people of Israel.)

Hispanics say, *"Mi casa es su casa,"* and devout Israelites said, "Your prayer is my prayer." We can imagine the development of a psalm. A person has had an intensely painful experience. In a community of prayer, he cries out to the Lord:

More numerous than the hairs on my head
are those who hate me without cause.
Those who attack me with lies
are too much for my strength.

His fellow Israelites realize that they cannot let this man pray alone, that their religion calls them to pray with him. His prayer becomes their prayer. The psalm is 69 and it contains so many poignant expressions of betrayal which are part of the human situation that it becomes recognized as an important prayer, one which must be offered now and preserved for generations to come. The prayer of one has become the prayer of everyone. When people come to understand the principle of solidarity they see why it is unnecessary to change "God, come to my assistance," to "God, come to our assistance." Because of our solidarity, there is no singular in authentic prayer.

A corollary of the concept of solidarity is the belief that liturgical celebration draws people of faith into the salvific event which is celebrated. Catholic liturgical scholars refer to this cultic reality as "anamnesis," living memorial, the "liturgical now." The past event which we remember liturgically occurs for us now spiritually but really. When we obey the command of Christ, "Do this in memory of me," we enter into the paschal mystery of his death and resurrection.

These principles of solidarity and anamnesis are exemplified in the great profession of faith in the Book of Deuteronomy.[3] Notice the easy transition from the singular to the plural and from the past to the present (remembering that the event described has occurred long before the people of Deuteronomy express their faith):

"A wandering Aramean was my father who went down to Egypt with a small household and lived there as an alien. But there he became a nation, great, strong, and numerous. When the Egyptians maltreated and oppressed us, imposing hard labor upon us, we cried to the Lord, the God of our fathers, and he heard our cry and saw our affliction, our

---

[3] Deuteronomy 26:5-9.

toil and our oppression. He brought us out of Egypt with his strong hand and outstretched arm, with terrifying power, with signs and wonders, and bringing us into this country, he gave us this land flowing with milk and honey."

Because of the principle of anamnesis, no psalm is lost in the historical setting of its composition. Every psalm comes alive because the original composition is held in the memory of God. Through anamnesis we enter into God's memory. Many years after the return from the exile, people prayed psalm 126 in their own name, even though they were not historically part of the original event:

> When the Lord delivered Zion from bondage,
> it seemed like a dream.
> Then was our mouth filled with laughter,
> on our lips there were songs.

Solidarity in Christ

When I pray psalm 17 I enter into a deeper understanding of solidarity.[4] This psalm of lament begins in a usual manner:

> Lord, hear a cause that is just,
> pay heed to my cry.
> Turn your ear to my prayer:
> no deceit is on my lips.

When I come to those words, "no deceit is on my lips," I have a hesitation. I am reluctant to make such a statement, and I feel even more reluctant as the psalm goes on:

> You search my heart, you visit me by night.
> You test me and you find in me no wrong.
> My words are not sinful as are men's words.

---

[4] See Daytime Prayer for Wednesday of Week I.

Frankly I feel embarrassed to say these things. I do not want to kid myself or try to deceive others about my innocence. The psalmist is, of course, protesting his innocence in a particular situation and that qualifies what he says. But there is a person who can say this psalm without any qualification; that person is Jesus. And pray the psalms Jesus did, not only in those few instances which are cited in the gospels, but throughout his life as a devout Jew. But what about all the other psalms, such as psalm 51 which, rather than protesting innocence, openly admits guilt: "Have mercy on me, God in your kindness. O wash me more and more from my guilt and cleanse me from my sin." Jesus could pray this psalm and others like it because he offered them to the Father in the person of his people. Just as the principle of solidarity urges us to see the suffering servant as the people of Israel, so an understanding of Christ urges us to see him as identified with the people who are the suffering servant.

St. Melito of Sardis (second century) in an Easter homily sees Christ as active even in those people who existed before his birth: "It is he who endured every kind of suffering in all those who foreshadowed him. In Abel he was slain, in Isaac bound, in Jacob exiled, in Joseph sold, in Moses exposed to die. He was sacrificed in the passover lamb, persecuted in David, and dishonored in the prophets."[5]

Jesus wishes to continue to pray the psalms in and through us, the members of his Mystical Body. Jesus the Christ, the Head of Humanity and of the Church, is the bond, the link with all other human beings. He is the source of our solidarity.

St. Therese of Lisieux, the Little Flower, searched for her vocation in the Church, her place in the Mystical Body. She said that when she had looked upon the Mystical Body of the Church, she recognized herself in none of the members which St. Paul described in the twelfth chapter of his first letter to the Corinthians. Through further reflection she realized that a body has a heart from which love flows,

---

[5] From the Office of Readings for Holy Thursday.

and that "love is everything." She then concluded, "In the heart of the Church, my mother, I will be love."[6]

Apostolic prayer calls us to be the love in the heart of the Mystical Body, and that love moves us to become the prayerful voice of Christ for the sake of all the members of his Body. Apostolic prayer is a fulfillment of the royal priesthood to which we have been called in the sacrament of baptism. The vocation of every member of the Church is to be a liturgist, not by becoming an expert in the study of liturgy, but by being someone who is dedicated to the corporate prayer of the Church.

To be involved in apostolic prayer does not mean that we abandon personal, individual prayer. In fact, as we shall see in the next chapter, apostolic prayer depends on personal, individual prayer and shows its necessity, but it does require that we understand that prayer is never an expression of self-love, that it is never narcissistic, and that we are required to expand our appreciation for prayer beyond what fits our needs and pleases our taste.

We will have made progress in a spirituality which is ecclesial and liturgical, that is, which is specifically Catholic and which understands the importance of the Church in our lives when prayer in the first place means corporate prayer, prayer which is offered through Christ in union with all of his members. This is apostolic prayer which adds a new dimension to what it means to come together in prayer.

---

[6] From her autobiography, as cited in the Office of Readings for October 1.

"Pray constantly and attentively for all in the holy company." (Ephesians 6:19)

Chapter Five

Private Prayer and Liturgical Prayer

"Pray to the Father in secret. . ." (Matthew 6:16)

I N THE ERA OF LITURGICAL RENEWAL which prepared for the Second Vatican Council, a few enthusiasts insisted that all we needed for a good prayer life was the celebration of the sacraments and the Divine Office. Devotions were judged to be superfluous, and liturgical prayer was considered to be entirely sufficient by itself. Not so, however for two priests whose story made the clerical rounds over thirty years ago. The two, mindful of the occupation of some of the apostles, were spending their day off fishing. Since the fish were not biting, they had both settled back to say the breviary when a sudden squall came up and threatened to capsize the boat. One of the priests, reaching for the oars, yelled in panic to the other, "Put away that book and start praying."

Whatever may be the quality of the humor of this anecdote, it does tend to illustrate that liturgical prayer does not meet every kind of human need, nor is it intended to do so. Liturgical prayer is community prayer which is designed to be a generous, outgoing, largely other-centered type of prayer. As community prayer it cannot possibly cater to the taste of each individual; as other-centered prayer it cannot always satisfy genuine personal needs. For a proper relationship with God we need both liturgical and private prayer, each in its own time and place.

What Is Prayer?

A very broad definition of prayer is that it is an expression of our relationship with God. It is communication, both to God and from God. It may be individual or it may be corporate. It may be silent or it may be spoken. We all need prayer which is individual as well as corporate, and which is silent as well as spoken.

One still hears some people complain, "I don't like the new Mass; I can't pray anymore." What this reflects is that previously people said personal, private prayers during Mass. The Mass for many provided a reverential atmosphere for individual prayer without inviting participation directly in the liturgy itself. Now with the return to the vernacular and active participation, people find no opportunity during the celebration of the Eucharist for personal devotions and intentions, an opportunity which must be found outside the liturgy. Liturgical prayer and private prayer are both necessary, and the one cannot supply for the other. Without liturgical prayer there is usually little growth toward a mature spirituality and there is insufficient sensitivity to the community nature of the Church. Without private prayer there is usually little opportunity for individual self-expression. Conscientious parents provide activities for the entire family as a group, but they also make opportunities for communication with each child individually. God our Father welcomes us into his home, the church, as his family, but he also invites each one of us to communicate with him individually in private.

Private Prayers Prepare for Liturgy

One vital aspect of private prayer is that it prepares for liturgical prayer. In the liturgy the primary orientation is to the Father through the Son in the unity of the Holy Spirit. Liturgical prayer is trinitarian, not in the sense that it will develop a "devotion" to each of three persons, but in the truth that it comes alive only in the awareness of our relationships to the persons of the Trinity. We are children of the Father, not of the Son or the Holy Spirit, and liturgical prayer is eminently the prayer of the Father's children. But this prayer is liturgical (and real) only and solely in union with Jesus Christ. He is the one who makes prayer liturgical, as we pray together with him. As others have already observed, the liturgy is not so much looking at the person of Jesus Christ as it is standing side by side with him and looking in the same direction as he, to the Father. Christ is our priest, our mediator, our intercessor with the Father.

When a family visited California, they made me think of Christ the priest. They flew into San Francisco and rented a car. After touring the city for several days and before driving south along the coast, they wanted to see the Golden Gate Bridge. This magnificent structure crosses the strait, some two miles wide, which links San Francisco Bay with the Pacific Ocean. When it was completed in 1937, its central span was the longest in the world. Perhaps more people have viewed this bridge in pictures, movies, and TV shows than any other bridge. And yet the bridge was built not to be admired, but to provide a safe and efficient means for traffic to cross from one side to the other, far above the not always tranquil waters of the bay.

Thinking about that experience with the Golden Gate Bridge helps us to understand the mission of God's Son when by the power of the Holy Spirit he took flesh and was born of the Virgin Mary. By his incarnation God's Son became our priest. Sin forged a chasm, separating us from God. By his incarnation Jesus spanned that chasm. He is our bridge to God. As Sacred Scripture attests, "There is one mediator between God and the human race, Christ Jesus, himself human, who gave himself as ransom for all" (1 Tm 2:5).

A bridge must reach to both shores. In his divinity Jesus is in contact with his Father. When he became human Jesus reached out to come into contact with us. The womb of Mary was like a cathedral in which her Son was anointed by the Holy Spirit as the great high priest. When the Son of God became the Son of Mary, he also became our priest, our bridge to God.

We must let Jesus be our priest, especially during all liturgical prayer. He earnestly desires to lift us far above the not always tranquil waters of life to be secure and sure as we approach the Father through, with, and in him, our great high Priest.

We are brought into union with Christ and moved to prayer through him by the loving force of the Holy Spirit, who makes us one in Christ. The liturgy presumes that we have an understanding and appreciation of the place of the Son and the Holy Spirit in our prayer to the Father. It is within private prayer and meditation that we develop this understanding and appreciation.

The Son Made Flesh

In baptism and confirmation we become conformed to the image of the Son. Our true identity is realized to the extent that we live out this initial conformity and celebrate it in the liturgy. To become truly ourselves, children of the Father, we must become conformed to the person of the Father's Son. But first we must know the Father's Son in whose image we are made. This image is not an abstraction. The Son has become flesh in Jesus Christ, someone we can and must identify with, someone who is human like us in all things but sin.

One aspect of private prayer should be a meditation on the humanity of Jesus Christ. In reflective reading of the Gospels we can come to know Christ Jesus in his varied human states as the early Christian communities of the four evangelists knew him. Reflections on the mysteries of Jesus Christ within the prayerful atmosphere of the rosary can also develop a warm intimacy with him. A sense of closeness and warmth with people depends on how well we know them, but usually we become closest to people when we share with them their time of crisis or sorrow. Personal prayer, then, should include loving reflection on the passion narratives of the Gospels, the praying of the sorrowful mysteries of the rosary, and the making of the stations of the cross. We must reflect on the entire mystery of Christ from his incarnation and birth through his resurrection and ascension, but we will most likely draw closest to Jesus Christ through attention to him in his time of crisis.

The Role of the Spirit

Love is a driving force, and the Holy Spirit is that force in the life of Jesus, moving him ever toward the Father. To fulfill our destiny we must be open to the Spirit. Most of us probably admit that we need time for peace and quiet to allow the Spirit to work within us. Average American adults ingest between ten and twenty thousand words a day in newspapers and magazines. We listen to the radio for about seventy-five minutes a day. We are awakened by a clock radio, we tune in while driving the car, and fall asleep at night as an automatic switch turns off the radio next to our bed. In addition we spend several hours each day watching television, more on the weekends. Battered as we are by almost ceaseless noise and distraction we need to de-stimulate our senses, and to lessen the constant flow of sound and images into a weary brain. We must not be afraid of silence, as we force ourselves to turn off the radio, the stereo, the television, and put down our newspapers and magazines, at least during some time of the day. We don't have to play the radio every time we get into the car. We don't have to have the TV on all evening. But we do have to search for solitude to think and to pray. In quiet we can extend the invitation, "Father, send forth your Holy Spirit."

Savoring the Liturgical Flavor

In order to catch the flavor of the trinitarian orientation of the liturgy, I can think of nothing better than a regular and reflective reading of the magnificent hymn found in Ephesians 1:3-14. This passage reveals why Jesus taught us to pray "Our Father," how we are one with Christ as children of the Father, and in what way the Spirit enters our lives. Another excellent passage is the entire eighth chapter of Romans. We should "take to heart these words and think of them at home and abroad, whether we are busy or at rest."

Progress in prayer can be derived from a diligent reading of the Gospel according to Luke. It is very much a Gospel of prayer. In it we hear Jesus present an extensive teaching on prayer and we witness his example of prayer. We also meet other prayerful people, particularly Mary, Zechariah, and Simeon, for it is from the prayers of these three people that the Church has taken its major canticles in the Liturgy of the Hours: the Magnificat at Evening Prayer, the Benedictus at Morning Prayer, and the Nunc Dimittis at Night Prayer.[1] Try reading Luke's Gospel all in one sitting. It is an unusually revealing and rewarding experience.

The Handmaid of Liturgical Prayer

Private prayer should lead to liturgical prayer. A violinist practices for hours alone, but all the individual effort is so that she may participate in the magnificent harmony of a symphony orchestra. Individual prayer is like that, even though it is not practice. A young professional ballplayer takes time every day during the winter to perfect his swing. He does so in order to be a productive member of his baseball team. Individual prayer is like that, even though it is not a game. Actors study their parts and memorize their lines. They do all that work so that they can be part of the play and interact with the other performers. Individual prayer is like that, even though it is not acting. All of this is not to minimize individual prayer but simply to apply the truth that "the liturgy is the summit toward which the activity of the Church is directed."

The Church warmly commends private devotions, but the Church also teaches us "that the liturgy by its very nature far surpasses any of them." Private devotions are the handmaid of liturgical prayer. A primary purpose of private prayer, then, is to lead to liturgical prayer. Indispensable is the guiding principle that the liturgy is indeed "the summit toward which all the activity of the Church is directed."[2]

---

[1] These prayers in English begin in order "My soul proclaims the greatness of the Lord," "Blessed be the Lord, the God of Israel," and "Lord, now you let your servant go in peace."

[2] See the *Constitution on the Sacred Liturgy*, nos. 10 and 13.

Taking Time With God

Celebrating the Mass and the Liturgy of the Hours daily together with additional attention to private prayer places a great demand on people and absorbs a considerable portion of their day. Is so much time necessary? Is it really practical? What good does it actually accomplish? Is it, in short, worth it? These may be good questions in most instances, but never dare ask them of two people who are in love concerning the time they spend with each other. When people are in love, being together is an end in itself. And if we could be open to the movement of the Spirit, the Spirit of love, we would cherish moments spent in prayer and we would yearn to pass more time with God. We would begin to live here on earth the life of our eternal destiny. Filled with the Holy Spirit and balanced by him between quietism and activism, our love for God would overflow into our love for others. Our days and our entire lives would indeed be made holy.

"Rejoice always, never cease praying, render constant thanks: such is God's will for you in Christ Jesus."
(1 Thessalonians 5:17)

CHAPTER SIX

More on Apostolic Prayer

"Glorify the Lord with me." (Psalm 34)

S OMETIMES A PRAYER STRIKES US as just right. It expresses our sentiments perfectly. I feel that way about psalm 27 which the Church presents in her prayer book at Evening Prayer for Wednesday of Week I.

This psalm begins, "The Lord is my light and my help; whom shall I fear? The Lord is the stronghold of my life; before whom shall I shrink?" I feel great confidence when I say that. Later in the psalm, I identify with a simple expression of longing: "It is your face, O Lord, that I seek."

I had been praying this psalm as part of the Divine Office since 1955 when one day a religious sister told me that it was her favorite psalm. She loved the expression of trust in the Lord, and she found particular meaning in this verse: "Though father and mother forsake me, the Lord will receive me." Her parents had opposed her vocation as a religious. She was an only child and her parents hoped she would give them grandchildren. It was not easy for her to keep her resolve to enter religious life. Now I think of her and many other people who have had to make hard decisions without family support, and I pray in their person as I say, "Do not abandon or forsake me, O God my help!"

This psalm also puts me in mind of people, most of them rather young, who have left the Church. For them and in their person I offer a prayer which I hope one day they will offer for themselves: "There is one thing I ask of the Lord, for this I long, to live in the house of the Lord all the days of my life, to savor the sweetness of the Lord, to behold his temple." I also pray in union with those parents who earnestly hope their children will return to the faith.

The conclusion of the psalm makes me think of those who are about to pass from this life to the next. Perhaps they are so ill that they cannot give voice to their prayer. I want to become their voice and say, "I am sure I shall see the Lord's goodness in the land of the living. Hope in him, hold firm and take heart. Hope in the Lord!"

The Heart of a Priest

My primary apostolate since my ordination has been to seminarians and priests. I have a loving concern for those priests who have left the active priesthood, each for his own reason. I have in mind a particular priest, much loved by his people and admired by both young and old among the clergy, who is now married, who for a while sold cars and who now works in a mortuary. Over lunch one day, he said to me, "I wish I could be both married and active in ordained ministry because I still have the heart of a priest." My priestly heart feels sadness for him and for all my priestly brothers who are no longer in active ministry. For them and in their persons I pray psalm 42:

> These things will I remember
> as I pour out my soul:
> how I would lead the rejoicing crowd
> into the house of God,
> amid cries of gladness and thanksgiving,
> the throng wild with joy.
> Why are you cast down, my soul,
> why groan within me?
> Hope in God; I will praise him still,
> my savior and my God.[1]

---

[1] Evening Prayer for Wednesday of Week II.

Psalm 43 used to be part of the prayers at the foot of the altar.[2] This psalm reminds me that I pray in union also with the priests who are continuing in active ministry, sometimes at no little cost to themselves emotionally and socially:

> Defend me, O God, and plead my cause
> against a godless nation.
> From deceitful and cunning men,
> rescue me, O God.
> O send forth your light and your truth;
> let these be my guide.
> Let them bring me to your holy mountain
> to the place where you dwell.
> And I will come to the altar of God,
> the God of my joy.

Psalm 38 Becomes Contemporary

Psalm 38 is a prayer of lament and in the old breviary it was listed among the penitential psalms.[3] It is the prayer of a person with a fatal illness which is not specified, although it is compared to leprosy. In that era few illnesses would be more dreaded than leprosy. In our day that distinction usually belongs to cancer. I find another application in the victims of AIDS, and I pray in their person:

> O Lord, do not rebuke me in your anger;
> do not punish me, Lord, in your rage.

Not all AIDS patient have contracted the disease by their own fault, and others may refuse to accept any guilt; I pray nevertheless in their person:

> My wounds are foul and festering,
> the result of my own folly.

---

[2] Psalm 43 is now prayed at Morning Prayer on Tuesday of Week II.
[3] Office of Readings for Friday of Week II.

I am bowed and brought to my knees.
I go mourning all the day long.
All my frame burns with fever;
all my body is sick.
Spent and utterly crushed,
I cry aloud in anguish of heart.
My friends avoid me like a leper;
those closest to me stand afar off.

I know of no more vivid image of AIDS, the modern disease, than these words of an ancient psalm. And so I continue with the prayer and I hope not only that I am voicing a prayer for many who have turned away from God, but also that I am in union with those who do cry out to God in their agony:

I count on you, O Lord;
it is you, Lord God, who will answer.
I pray, "Do not let them mock me,
those who triumph if my foot should slip."

I add the earnest conclusion:

O Lord, do not forsake me!
My God, do not stay afar off!
Make haste and come my help.
O Lord, my God, my Savior!

This psalm is found in the Office of Readings for Fridays of Week II. It is also part of the Office of Readings for Good Friday. When I pray this psalm on Good Friday, I am reminded that in his passion and death Jesus drew all people to himself, lifted them up, and offered them in loving sacrifice to his heavenly Father. That yearly experience helps me to realize not only that Jesus identified himself with all human suffering, but that every psalm is to be prayed in union with and for his people.

A Little Girl and a Young Man

Some years ago I learned of a little girl who was in a hospital, dying of leukemia. She told her mother that she did not want to go to sleep at night because she was afraid she would not wake up. Since then, I do not think I have failed to remember her, and to pray in the person of many people like her, when I say in psalm 143 at Tuesday Night Prayer:

> In the morning let me know your love
> for I put my trust in you.

In 1991 a former seminarian committed suicide. On his desk in his room his parents found his Liturgy of the Hours opened to psalm 86 at Monday Night Prayer. In his last desperate moments, confused and depressed, he seemed to have been struggling to reach out to God with a hope that at least God would understand:

> Turn your ear, O Lord, and give answer
> for I am poor and needy.
> Preserve my life, for I am faithful:
> save the servant who trusts in you.

As I follow along in this prayer I sense a loss of his resolve to continue the struggle but still with trust in God's mercy:

> O Lord, you are good and forgiving,
> full of love to all who call.
> In the day of distress I will call
> and surely you will reply.

In a fatal moment of inscrutable and final agony, he put a gun to his head and pulled the trigger. Even for that violent and instant transition from this world to the next, psalm 86 supplies a fervent and confident prayer:

> I will praise you, Lord my God, with all my heart
> and glorify your name for ever;
> for your love to me has been great:
> you have saved me from the depths of the grave.

One statistical study indicates that the highest incidence of suicide in the United States is between the ages of fourteen and twenty-five. This former seminarian was twenty-four. I feel an urgent call to pray in the person of these many young people, but I cannot forget those whom they leave behind. How can parents endure such a tragedy? How can they and friends overcome the almost inevitable feelings of guilt: "What did we do wrong, what more should we have done?" With them in mind I continue to pray within the same psalm:

> But you, God of mercy and compassion,
> slow to anger, O Lord,
> abounding in love and truth,
> turn and take pity on me.

On a Happier Note

Apostolic prayer seems particularly appropriate in poignant situations, but it applies to all human experiences, including uplifting and happy ones. I want to heed the invitation of those who pray psalm 34:

> Glorify the Lord with me.
> Together let us praise his name.[4]

I love the jubilance of psalm 149 and I join with happy people whose prayer fulfills the sentiments of this psalm:

> Sing a new song to the Lord,
> his praise in the assembly of the faithful.

---

[4] Saturday Daytime Prayer in Weeks I and III.

> Let Israel rejoice in its maker,
> let Zion's sons exult in their king.
> Let them praise his name with dancing
> and make music with timbrel and harp.
> For the Lord takes delight in his people.
> He crowns the poor with salvation.[5]

The Wedding Song of the King

Wedding bells signal a happy event, as long as a shotgun is not involved. The Book of Psalms is not without a wedding song. Psalm 45 celebrates the marriage of an Israelite king to a foreign princess.[6] The identity of the king for whose wedding the psalm was first composed is not at all certain. After kings no longer reigned in Israel, the psalm was retained and applied to the king who was to come, the anointed one, the Messiah. Now the Church sees this psalm as fulfilled in Christ the King who has taken the Church as his royal bride.

While never losing sight of the messianic interpretation, I personally like to pray this psalm in union with couples who are entering upon a life together in the sacrament of marriage. A man is never more handsome than on his wedding day, as the psalmist proclaims to the groom:

> You are the fairest of the children of men
> and graciousness is poured upon your lips:
> because God has blessed you for evermore.

Every woman on her wedding day is like a princess in her loveliness:

> The daughter of the king is clothed with splendor,
> her robes embroidered with pearls set in gold.
> She is led to the king with her maiden companions.
> They are escorted amid gladness and joy.

---

[5] Sunday Morning Prayer in Week I.
[6] Monday Evening Prayer in Week II and Saturday Daytime Prayer in Week IV.

Even though she must leave her family in order to take a husband, the new bride is given a beautiful promise:

> Sons shall be yours in place of your fathers:
> you will make them princes over all the earth.

The psalm concludes with a prayer for fidelity, for a life-long relationship which becomes a model for other couples, an example worthy of admiration:

> May this song make your name for ever remembered.
> May the peoples praise you from age to age.

When I pray this wedding song, I reflect on the union of love which marriage is, and I see its application to the union of Christ and his Church.

Weddings are happy events, and I am pleased to be part of them through prayer. I also like to join happy people in other aspects of their lives which are expressed in prayer, and especially to be one with them in the joy they proclaim because of their dedication to God's will. Psalm 119 is the longest of all the psalms, with 176 verses.[7] It begins on a joyful note:

> They are happy whose life is blameless,
> who follow God's law.
> They are happy who do his will,
> seeking him with all their hearts.

These initial verses reflect the theme established in the very first psalm:

> Happy indeed is the man
> who follows not the counsel of the wicked,
> but whose delight is the law of the Lord
> and who ponders his law day and night.[8]

---

[7] This psalm in the Liturgy of the Hours is divided into twenty-two sections of eight verses each and spread throughout the four weeks of the month; it is prayed primarily at Daytime Prayer.

[8] Office of Readings for Sunday of Week I.

Perspective on Prayer and Action

When I get enthusiastic about prayer, I try to maintain a proper perspective. Spiritual writers are quick to admonish us not to adopt the position that our work is our prayer; on the other hand, we do need to see equally that prayer does not substitute for ministry. In fact, authentic prayer should lead to action. The great liturgical reformers, especially those who were inspired in the United States by Father Virgil Michel, O.S.B., were convinced that Catholics would be moved to extensive social action through the liturgical renewal. That conversion takes place, I think, in the degree in which we go beyond the mere externals of liturgy to a profound dedication to the liturgy as corporate prayer, the prayer of Christ in union with his Body for the sake of the whole world, a prayer which can be termed "apostolic."

Ministry is not a substitute for prayer, nor is prayer a substitute for ministry. A proper perspective does show us, however, that apostolic prayer will lead to ministry, and that ministry will direct us back to apostolic prayer. Circumstances determine where emphasis needs to be placed, whether on prayer or action, but I suspect that in many instances we fail to value prayer as we ought. Imagine the scene in a hospital when family and friends are gathered around the bed of a loved one who is dying. A doctor has said that all medical means have been exhausted. One of the family members says, "I guess all we can do now is pray." Prayer seems to be a last resort when all else has failed, but it should be the first effort we make. Sometimes when people thank me for having prayed with them, I am tempted to say, "That is the least I can do," but then I remember that it is really the most I can do.

Apostolic prayer, I am convinced, will give us the balance we need. This kind of prayer includes all human sentiments and every human need. And so the Liturgy of the Hours invites us, whether we are happy or sad, hopeful or discouraged, to come before God in union with his Son, together in prayer.

"Pray for one another that you may find healing."
(James 5:16)

Part II
THE HOURS

"By a tradition going back to the earliest Christian times, the divine office is arranged so that the whole course of the day is made holy by the praises of God."

(Constitution on the Liturgy, no. 84)

"Pray for those who mistreat you."
(Luke 6:28)

CHAPTER SEVEN

Together in Prayer Throughout the Day

*"Glorify the Lord with me; together let us
praise his name." (Psalm 34)*

ON THURSDAY SEPTEMBER 28, 1978 I was watching the late news on TV when they announced that a bulletin had just come from Rome: Pope John Paul I was dead. I couldn't believe it. The man had been Pope, I thought to myself, for only about a month (thirty-three days, to be exact). He seemed to be a bright ray of hope for the Church, a pastoral man full of love for God and his people. After his election he stood on the balcony of St. Peter's to give his blessing, he looked at the vast crowd of cheering people, and he smiled. He seemed to be everyone's idea of a grandfather. And now he was dead? There had to be some mistake. It could not be. But there was no mistake. The Pope was dead.

I was distressed. I was disturbed and upset. I paced up and down in my room. I said, "God, why have you done this to us?" But then I realized that the next day would be a busy one, and that I had to go to bed and get some rest, no matter what. Before retiring I sat down in my chair, opened my Liturgy of the Hours to Night Prayer for Thursday and this is what I found in psalm 16:

> I say to the Lord, "You are my God.
> My happiness lies in you alone."

He has put into my heart a marvelous love
for the faithful ones who dwell in his land.

I thought: that is a portrait of Pope John Paul I. I went on in the
prayer:

O Lord, it is you who are my portion and cup;
it is you yourself who are my prize.
The lot marked out for me is my delight:
welcome indeed the heritage that falls to me.
And so my heart rejoices, my soul is glad,
even my body shall rest in safety,
for you will not leave my soul among the dead,
nor let your beloved know decay.

I then reflected that we received the bulletin in California on
Thursday night when it was already Friday morning in Rome. This
meant that the Pope had gone to bed on a Thursday. Like a good priest,
he had said Night Prayer before he retired. His last prayer on this earth
was psalm 16, which I was offering in my room that unforgettable
night. That realization gave me an intense feeling of unity with the
Pope, of oneness with him in his final prayer which completed his life
in this world with trust in God to whom he said:

You will show me the path of life,
the fullness of joy in your presence,
at your right hand happiness for ever.

The experience was deeply moving for me, and it convinced me
of the value of praying the Liturgy of the Hours faithfully every day. The
prayer of the Church brings me into union with innumerable men and
women all around the world and with those in whose person they pray
in an apostolic spirit.

When I gave a workshop on the Liturgy of the Hours to the sisters
and priests of the diocese of Juneau, Alaska I was impressed by their
dedication and their spirit of self-sacrifice, living alone for the most part,

separated from one another by the vastness of the area, and subject to the deep intensity of the cold, long, dark winters. I urged them to be united with each other in the prayer of the Church and to find strength through offering the same prayer, even though they were separated by many miles from each other.

During my brief stay, despite the awesome beauty of the region, I begin to feel a sense of aloneness, almost of desolation. On a Wednesday night when it had already been dark for a long time, I entered into a new understanding of psalm 130 at Night Prayer:

> Out of the depths I cry to you, O Lord,
> Lord, hear my voice!
> My soul is waiting for the Lord,
> I count on his word.
> My soul is longing for the Lord
> more than watchmen for daybreak.

Since that experience I continue to pray this psalm on Wednesday nights in the person of the people of Alaska, especially those who also offer the prayer of the Church.

Obligation and Choice

I think it would be very pleasing to God the Father, as well as beneficial to his children, if all the people of the Church were to join Christ in the offering of this daily liturgical prayer. First are the ordained members of the Church, bishops, priests, and deacons. Canon 276 states that "priests as well as deacons aspiring to the priesthood are obliged to fulfill the Liturgy of the Hours daily." During the ceremony of ordination, the candidates for holy orders make a solemn promise to offer this prayer each day. Every Saturday at Night Prayer we are reminded of the call to offer the prayer of the Church:

> O come, bless the Lord,
> all you who serve the Lord,

who stand in the house of the Lord,
in the courts of the house of our God.

But through baptism we are all servants of the Lord, and we are all called to a ministry of prayer, especially the perennial prayer of the Church, the Liturgy of the Hours.

Making Holy the Day

First in Catholic piety even before the Liturgy of the Hours must be the Mass. The celebration of the Eucharist is the center of Catholic life. It is the heartbeat of the Church. But the Eucharist, although communicating its life-giving grace throughout the entire day, consumes only a brief period of time. In order to sanctify the entire day, the Church distributes the Liturgy of the Hours over the entire time of our waking moments. That is why it is called "the Hours."

Morning Prayer, formerly known as Lauds from its Latin name, comes first. It should be the initial prayer of the day, offered as soon after rising as possible. It is one of the two major prayers of the Liturgy of the Hours, the other being Evening Prayer or Vespers.

Evening Prayer is to be offered before or after the evening meal, approximately at that time when Jesus met with his disciples for the passover celebration on the night before he died.

Daytime Prayer spans the gap between Morning and Evening Prayer. It contains selections which are to be chosen according to whether the prayer is offered in mid-morning, midday, or mid-afternoon.

The Office of Readings may be prayed at any convenient time when we can find a few moments for a reflective, meditative type of prayer.

Night Prayer closes out the day as the last prayer before sleep. These are the five divisions of the Church's prayer for each day of the year. My considered estimate is that a very devout praying of these five divisions consumes no more than forty-five minutes. The idea, however, is not to sit down and pray them all at once. Their purpose is to sanctify the day at its beginning, at its middle, at its twilight, and at its conclusion.

Catholics who do not as yet have the practice of using the Church's prayer book can incorporate the five parts of the prayer gradually into their routine. It is good to begin with either Morning Prayer or Evening Prayer, and then to add the other of these major prayers as soon as possible. I suggest that Night Prayer be chosen next; it is brief and easy to grasp in its theme. The fourth prayer to be chosen can be Daytime Prayer. Last of all is the Office of Readings.

Three Fallacies

Sister Janet Baxendale, S.C. of New York, a strong advocate of the Liturgy of the Hours, observes that there are three fallacies which interfere with the effort to get Catholics to use the prayer book of the Church. The first fallacy states that if the Office is not sung it should not be celebrated publicly. The second states that if the Office is not prayed with others, it is better not to pray it at all. The third states that the number of psalms in Morning or Evening Prayer ought to be reduced because they constitute "too much prayer." She rejects all three fallacies and hopes they will be discarded without further ado.[1]

Praying the Liturgy of the Hours alone is a good thing to do when we cannot find someone to pray with. It is better to join with others, even with two or three. It is best to celebrate the hours with ceremony and music. But we must not let the better and the best become the enemy of the good. Even when an ideal form of celebration cannot be achieved, it is still desirable and beneficial to pray the hours alone since through Christ we are united with others. Sometimes people worry about whether they are saying the prayer "right" according to the directives. The important thing is to pray. "Rightness" can come later. And when we understand the rhythmic arrangement of each of the

---

[1] See her article in *America*, Vol. 162, No. 9, "The Best-Kept Secret of Liturgical Reform."

hours, we will be eager to pray them as they are arranged without reducing the number of psalms or omitting the canticles.[2]

Some days can be particularly hectic. In those situations it may seem impossible to pray all five parts. Emphasis in that case should be put on Morning and Evening Prayer. If the time for Evening Prayer has passed, then select Night Prayer. Catholic piety does call us, however, to make time for prayer each day. It is not too much to ask that devout Catholics will eventually make the entire Liturgy of the Hours a regular part of their day.

I yearn for the day when Catholics, who are invited to some gathering, can be told, "Bring your prayer book," and they will know that means the Liturgy of the Hours. I maintain a hope that through this prayer Catholics will have a sense of intense union with Christ and through him with each other.

Individualism and Narcissism

To Sister Janet Baxendale's consideration of three fallacies about liturgical prayer, I add two obstacles. The first is the strong inclination to make religion private, an individual matter between God and me, a kind of spiritual honeymoon from which others are excluded. There is an individual aspect to religion, but it can never exclude our calling to be part of the people of God. Repeatedly without ever succumbing to tedium we must recall and strive to live by the central idea of the Second Vatican Council: "It has pleased God to save us and to make us holy, not merely as individuals without any mutual bonds, but by forming us into a single people who worship him in truth and who serve him in holiness."[3] Individualism is the opposite of the principle of solidarity.

---

[2] Sometimes when only one psalm is employed at Evening Prayer there is an appeal to "Cathedral Vespers" as opposed to "Monastic Vespers," as if we have written records of precisely how Evening Prayer was celebrated pastorally by people before the influence of monasticism complicated the Office. Most early forms of popular or "Cathedral" Vespers employed favorite psalms which were used consistently and without any attempt at variety, but the purpose was not to abbreviate prayer.

[3] Previously cited in Chapter 4.

The second great obstacle is spiritual narcissism, a false kind of self-love which makes my own pleasure and satisfaction the norm for the validity of religious experience. We cannot always fault immature youngsters for complaining that the Mass is boring, not only because sometimes the manner of celebration is inept but because it is the nature of youth to be pre-occupied with themselves, to spend hours in the front of a mirror appraising and adjusting their appearance (that includes boys as well as girls). Maturity tends to change, or at least lessen, that tendency of youth. Spiritual maturity requires that when we look in the mirror we see the image of Christ, and that when we see others, despite any appearances which may suggest the contrary, we recognize that they bear the same image. With them we form one people who worship God in truth and who serve him in holiness.

There is a lesson to be learned in the fact that for many of us our favorite psalm is 23 ("The Lord is my shepherd. There is nothing I shall want") and not psalm 88 ("Friend and neighbor you have taken away. My one companion is darkness"). There is nothing wrong with being comforted by the image of the Good Shepherd provided we also remember that Christ is the one who, in his passion, became the person whose one companion was darkness and who continues to identify, as we should, with those who feel that friend and neighbor have been taken from them.

A Prayer for Transformation

Union with Christ in the psalms is what makes our prayer pleasing to the Father, and union with Christ in our lives is what makes that kind of prayer possible. A young Vincentian priest, John Gabriel Perboyre, C.M., earnestly wished to become a missionary to China. Instead he was made the director of novices. In one of his conferences he said, "Let us keep our eyes fixed on Jesus Christ. Let us not content ourselves with catching one or two traits of our model, but let us enter into all his sentiments, let us acquire all his virtues." His superiors decided to grant his wish to leave his home in France to evangelize the poor of China. His mission was immediately successful. He made many converts and developed a strong Christian community. But then a terrible persecution broke out. The government was determined to rid the country of foreigners and to crush the Church. John Gabriel and most of his people went underground until they were betrayed by one of their own. John Gabriel was arrested. He was dragged from one tribunal to another and then was imprisoned for about six months before he was condemned to death. He was taken from his cell and led to a hill where on a Friday afternoon he was strangled to death while hanging from a cross. The year was 1840.

When Pope Leo XIII beatified John Gabriel on November 10, 1899, he commented on the remarkable similarity between the sufferings and death of this humble priest and that of his Lord, Jesus Christ. It so happened that after the death of John Gabriel, his confreres discovered among his papers a prayer which he had composed. This is the prayer:

O my divine Savior, transform me into yourself.
May my hands be the hands of Jesus.
May my tongue be the tongue of Jesus.
Grant that every faculty of my body
may serve only to glorify you.
Above all, transform my soul and all its powers
that my memory, my will, and my affections
may be the memory, the will, and the affections of Jesus.
I pray you to destroy in me all that is not of you.
Grant that I may live but in you and by you and for you,
and that I may truly say with St. Paul,
"I live, now not I, but Christ lives in me."

This prayer is most appropriate, I believe, during the quiet moments after having received holy communion. The answer to this prayer, which takes a lifetime to complete, disposes us to pray as we ought in an apostolic spirit in union with Christ and all his members.

When I am tempted to skip part or even all of the day's Liturgy of the Hours, I try to remember that Christ is eager to pray within me. He wants to have a kind of new incarnation through me. I make the effort to stir up my faith to recognize that Christ is the one standing before his Father in heaven but looking back at us and saying, "Glorify the Lord with me. Together let us praise his name."

"If anyone among you is suffering hardship, he must pray." (James 5:13)

Chapter Eight

Morning Prayer

"My mouth will proclaim your praise." (Psalm 51:17)

S OME PEOPLE AWAKEN AND SAY, "Good morning, God." Others awaken and say, "Good God! Morning!" Some of us are morning people, and others of us are night people. It has been said that the Church is run by morning people who have surrounded early rising with an aura of sanctity, but not everyone is enthusiastic about the austerity involved in abandoning a warm, comfortable bed. A survey has shown that the amount of sleep the average person needs is twenty minutes more. That is why electric alarm clocks have a snooze button. Who among us feels like jumping out of bed and shouting the words of psalm 57: "Awake, my soul, awake, lyre and harp, I will awake the dawn"?

Leaving aside the question of whether there is special virtue in early rising, the Church hopes that in our first waking moments we will offer praise to God in the sentiments of psalm 5:

> It is you whom I invoke, O Lord.
> In the morning you hear me;
> in the morning I offer you my prayer,
> watching and waiting.

Morning Prayer should be the first prayer of the day as soon after rising as reasonable. Its theme is the praise of God, a theme indicated by the Latin name, Lauds. The theme is explicit as the prayer begins. The presider says, "Lord, open my lips," and the community responds, "And my mouth will proclaim your praise."[1] (Thanksgiving is included in this meaning of praise.)

Morning Prayer is composed of a psalm, an Old Testament canticle, and a second psalm. It is the second psalm which emphasizes the theme. It is the keynote psalm, and it is always a prayer of praise. Frequently the first word we say is "praise," as in psalm 150 for Sunday of Week II: "Praise God in his holy place." Or the word "praise" appears early in the prayer as in psalm 149 for Sunday of Week I: "Sing a new song to the Lord, / his praise in the assembly of the faithful." Psalms of thanksgiving are also assigned to Morning Prayer because they are essentially the same as psalms of praise. Actually all the psalms are in a sense songs of praise, but the twenty-three different ones which have been selected as the second psalm for Morning Prayer present a special emphasis on praise as their theme.

The Meaning of Praise

Why the emphasis on praise? What about love? Isn't the love of God the greatest commandment, together with the love of neighbor, as Jesus forcefully taught us? Love is not a simple matter. It takes many forms: the love of spouses for one another, the love of parents for their children and of children for their parents, the love between friends, the love of teachers and helpers for their charges. There is the love of fidelity, the love of devotion, the love of delight, the love of compassion. Liturgical praise is a special kind of love. It expresses love for someone who is God. It is love imbued with admiration. This kind of love we call worship.

---

[1] Sometimes the Office of Readings precedes Morning Prayer. In that case, the Office of Readings is introduced by the words "Lord, open my lips," and the response, "And my mouth will proclaim your praise" so that praise is the first sentiment offered to God as the day begins. Only when the first prayer is one other than Morning Prayer is it necessary to offer the Invitatory Psalm.

To praise God means to recognize his power, to appreciate his goodness, to esteem his wisdom, to cherish his love, to marvel at his mystery. Perhaps the best word to associate with praise is "acknowledgment." To acknowledge the qualities of God is to praise him. That is why in the Fourth Eucharistic Prayer we offer praise to God by saying, "Father, we acknowledge your greatness." Then we add: "All your actions show your wisdom and love." The reason for this liturgical emphasis on actions is that the biblical understanding of God is not drawn from philosophical abstractions. The Bible does much more than tell us that God is powerful, good, wise, loving, and mysterious. The biblical presentation follows the truth that actions speak louder than words. Although the human mind can come to a knowledge of God in himself through the light of reason, the God of revelation makes himself known through his actions in salvation history. Very helpful, then, for our understanding of the meaning of praise are these remarkable words of the Fourth Eucharistic Prayer which summarize the meaning of praise: "Father, we acknowledge your greatness. All your actions show your wisdom and love."

This Eucharistic Prayer continues by declaring before God what he has done: "You formed man and woman in your own likeness and entrusted the whole world to their care. . . . Even when they disobeyed you and lost your friendship, you did not abandon them to the power of death, but extended your hand in mercy, that all who search for you might find you. Again and again you offered humankind a covenant and through the prophets nurtured the hope of salvation. Father, you so loved the world that in the fullness of time you sent your only Son to be our Savior."[2] The prayer then goes on to proclaim before the Father the actions of his Son on our behalf.

The way in which the Holy Spirit has revealed God in the Bible has shaped the nature of liturgical worship. We praise and thank God by telling him what he has done. Consider a typical Preface of the Eucharistic Prayer: "Father, it is our duty and our salvation always and

---

[2] From the proposed ICEL text, awaiting approval as of this writing in 1994.

everywhere to give you thanks through your beloved Son, Jesus Christ.
He is the Word through whom you made the universe, the Savior you
sent to redeem us. By the power of the Holy Spirit he took flesh and
was born of the Virgin Mary. For our sake he opened his arms on the
cross; he put an end to death and revealed the resurrection. In this he
fulfilled your will and won for you a holy people."[3] God knows that he
has done all these things in Christ his Son. We are not informing him
in case he has failed to recognize his own wonders; rather in proclaiming his marvelous works among us, we are proclaiming his praise.

The psalms of praise and thanks, then, recount God's works,
sometimes directly to God as we do within our eucharistic prefaces,
sometimes only in his presence. A splendid example is psalm 33 which
is proclaimed to the community in the presence of God the creator:

> Ring our your joy to the Lord, O you just;
> his praise is fitting for loyal hearts.
> By his word the heavens were made,
> by the breath of his mouth all the stars.
> He collects the waves of the ocean;
> he stores up the depths of the sea.[4]

We follow this same style of narrative praise and thanksgiving in
our dealings with each other. We thank people, as well as praise them,
by telling them what they do well. We thank and praise a cook by saying
something like, "You make the best ham loaf in the world and your
mustard sauce is simply unsurpassed."

Eucharist is Thanks and Praise

In thinking further about the meaning of praise, it is helpful to
reflect on the word "eucharist," a Greek word which means "to give

---

[3] From the Second Eucharistic Prayer, based on the prayer of the Roman priest, Hippolytus,
which was composed around the year 210 A.D.
[4] See Morning Prayer for Tuesday of Week I.

thanks." The Church has traditionally understood this word as having a deeper meaning than simply a response of gratitude for a favor received. In liturgy it reflects a usage of the Jews who, as we have seen, did not have a word for "thanksgiving." To thank God meant to praise and glorify him, to bless his name. Such is the meaning of the *benedixit* in the Latin formula of the consecration at Mass, which is quite correctly rendered in English as "he gave you thanks and praise." While we must offer gratitude to God for personal favors, we should learn to see that even small gifts are a sign of God's goodness which is worthy of our praise.

The story of the ten lepers in Luke's Gospel (17:11-19) illustrates the linking of praise and thanksgiving. The one leper "came back praising God in a loud voice." Jesus interpreted that praise as a form of thanksgiving when he asked, "Was there no one to return and give thanks to God except this foreigner?"[5]

In the Preface of the Eucharistic Prayer we profess that it is right always and everywhere to give thanks to God. It is especially right to begin the day by offering thanks and praise to God in our Morning Prayer.

The First Psalm

The first psalm of Morning Prayer has been chosen because of its suitability to the beginning of the day. Such suitability must be interpreted broadly. Sometimes the psalm refers to dawn or morning as in psalm 5 for Monday Morning Prayer in Week I:

> It is you whom I invoke, O Lord,
> in the morning you hear me;
> in the morning I offer you my prayer,
> watching and waiting.

---

[5] Actually there is only one word in the Greek text for both the Samaritan's expression and Jesus' response. That word means "to glorify" and from it we have derived our word, "doxology." I think, however, that the translator was correct in interpreting the first use of the word as "praise" and in the second as "thanks" because of the context.

The same is true of psalm 92 which is found at Saturday Morning Prayer of Week II:

> It is good to give thanks to the Lord,
> to make music to your name, O Most High,
> to proclaim your love in the morning.

Often psalms of lament or petition have been chosen. Of the twenty-eight possibilities for this initial psalm over four weeks, fourteen of the selections are prayers of lament. These prayers place us in the human predicament as the waking day begins. They remind us how much both we and others need God. They also call us out of ourselves to enter the world of those who are in need, and to pray in the apostolic spirit. Psalm 42 is a typical morning prayer of lament. From within those people in union with whom we pray, we cry out:

> Why are you cast down, my soul,
> why groan within me?
> Hope in God; I will praise him still,
> my savior and my God.

The other choices for the first psalm are various hymns and songs of praise and thanksgiving in accord with the Church's idea of what Morning Prayer should be.

Old Testament Theme

Between the two psalms of Morning Prayer the liturgy places one of the Old Testament canticles. These canticles are hymns to God drawn from books of the Bible other than that of the psalms. The use of these canticles is based on the fact that the early morning hour suggests the theme of Old Testament salvation history. At the beginning of the day we celebrate the beginnings of God's plan. God's providential movements in history are important to us in the Christian era. As Pope Pius XI pointed out, we are all spiritually Semites;

Abraham is our father in faith. The coming of Christ is a fulfillment of the covenant made with Abraham, and the entire Old Testament is a salvific action of God which reaches its climax in the person of Jesus Christ. Nor are God's actions buried in the past. We are united with the chosen of the Old Testament as the people of God and share with them God's loving kindness toward them. Christians should identify with the "we," the "our," and the "us" in the following verses from psalm 126:

> When the Lord delivered Zion from bondage,
> it seemed like a dream.
> Then was our mouth filled with laughter,
> on our lips there were songs.
> The heathens themselves said: "What marvels
> the Lord worked for them!"
> What marvels the Lord worked for us!
> Indeed we are glad.

God is one and the same in the Old and the New Testament eras. The God of Israel is the God of Christians. The God of Abraham is the Father of our Lord Jesus Christ:

> Lord, you have been our refuge
> from one generation to the next.
> Before the mountains were born
> or the earth or the world brought forth,
> you are God, without beginning or end (Psalm 90).

The Canticle of Zechariah

The Old Testament theme reaches both its high point and its perspective in the canticle of Zechariah (the *Benedictus*) which is used in every Morning Prayer.[6] The name, "Zechariah," literally means "God has remembered," and is symbolic of God's keeping his promises

---

[6] Further comments on Zechariah's canticle can be found at the end of Chapter 15.

made in the Old Testament. This hymn resounds with Old Testament allusions: David, the prophets, Abraham, the covenant. God is indeed to be blessed and praised because he has remembered all his promises to his people, promises of which the Baptist, son of Zechariah, is the last prophet in a long line of outstanding people raised up by God to carry his plan forward to the day of Christ.

The Resurrection Theme

The Church does not celebrate Old Testament themes as if Christ has not yet died and been raised to the glory of God the Father. Zechariah's canticle helps give perspective to Old Testament themes. It is a Gospel canticle (that is why it is prayed standing and why the sign of the cross is made as it begins) which lifts us in an instant to the fulfillment of the ancient covenant with Abraham. That fulfillment is Christ's resurrection which is symbolized by the dawn. Only in English do we have a theological pun: the rising sun is a symbol of the risen Son:

> In the tender compassion of our God
> the dawn from on high shall break upon us,
> to shine on those who dwell in darkness
> and the shadow of death,
> and to guide our feet into the way of peace.

Consecration of the Day

While the Church obviously intends that we begin our day with the praise of God, it does not entirely neglect the popular orientation toward a petition for help during the day. Following the canticle of Zechariah, the Church gives us a series of invocations whose primary, although not exclusive, purpose is to consecrate the day to God. Some typical petitions are:

> Let your splendor rest upon us today,
> direct the work of our hands.

> Give us your eternal wisdom,
> to be with us today and to guide us.

But intentions for the welfare of others are not excluded:

> Look kindly on all who put their trust in our prayers,
> fill them with every bodily and spiritual grace.[7]

These petitions lead to the first of the three official times the Church prays the "Our Father" daily (the other two are at Mass and Evening Prayer). Morning Prayer concludes with a collect type prayer such as that found at Mass. The fullness of the Christian theme is expressed in the trinitarian conclusion of this prayer: "We ask this through our Lord Jesus Christ, your Son, who lives and reigns with you and the Holy Spirit, one God, for ever and ever."

Preserving the Spirit of Morning Prayer

Every effort should be made to celebrate Morning Prayer as the first prayer of the day. Before we undertake any work or other human activity we should present ourselves to God in the spirit of psalm 5:

> It is you whom I invoke, O Lord.
> In the morning you hear me;
> in the morning I offer you my prayer,
> watching and waiting.

Even an early morning Mass ideally should be preceded by Morning Prayer, and it is worth the effort to rise promptly for the sake of this prayer. Although the General Instruction allows for a combining of Morning Prayer with Mass, it seems better to keep the two distinct. The reason is that they have entirely different purposes. Morning Prayer sanctifies the first moments of the day, whereas Mass is the culmination of the entire day no matter when it is celebrated.

---

[7] Selected from the petitions for Monday and Tuesday Morning Prayer for Week I.

The Church has never apologized for its predilection for the praise of God, nor need it do so now in a busy, task-oriented world. We are made to sing the praises of God for all eternity and that destiny begins here on this earth. God has no need of our praise, it is true, and our prayer adds nothing to his greatness; rather we are the ones who grow to fulfillment through a life of praise.[8] God is good to predestine us to praise his glory, to be conformed to the image of his Son whose entire life was a priestly life of praise of his Father. This praise should have, as it did for Jesus, all the tender affection of a child for a good father. Our praise is the expression of love for someone who is God.

Happy and holy is the day which begins with the Church's Morning Prayer of praise.

---

[8] Preface for Weekdays IV.

CHAPTER NINE

Evening Prayer

"Praised be the God and Father of Our Lord Jesus Christ."
(Ephesians 1:3)

T HE PROPER TIME FOR EVENING PRAYER, or Vespers, is the very late afternoon or early evening when the day is drawing to a close. To capture the spirit of Evening Prayer is not easy in our busy modern world. For earlier generations the hours of darkness meant rest from work, quiet relaxation, a time to sit peacefully and read or simply reflect, but for us the day is often far from over when evening comes. The anxieties and tensions of the working hours intrude upon the evening with little respect for our instinctive yearning for peace and calm. Effort will be needed not only to set aside time for Vespers but also to learn to consecrate the preoccupations and worries of the day through prayer so that we may spend precious moments with God and each other in celebrating his loving kindness manifested in the person and mission of Jesus Christ.

The Theme of Fullness

The great Christian revelation is that God literally has a Son, born in eternity before time began. The hour for Vespers, when the day is at its full, sets the theme: the fullness of time when God sent his Son. As Morning Prayer is a celebration of Old Testament revelation leading to Christ, so Evening Prayer is a celebration of the fullness of revelation in the New Testament. Every Vespers is situated in the supper hour when Jesus, having loved his own who were in the world, showed the depth of his love.[1]

Each Evening Prayer is composed of two psalms and two New Testament canticles. Twelve of the psalms selected are royal psalms, commemorating events which have their setting in the experience of a king. These royal psalms as prayed by the Church are understood in the light of further revelation which brings the person of Christ the King into sharper focus as the fulfillment of kingship in Israel. Other Vesper psalms are the Great Hallel Psalms (120-136), which include psalms thought to have been the prayer of pilgrims as they went up to Jerusalem for the liturgical feasts of Israel. The designation, "Hallel" (as in "Halleluia") has also been used for psalms 111-118. Jewish families often sang psalms 113 and 114 before the seder meal and 115-118 afterward. It seems likely that Jesus and his disciples sang all or parts of psalms 115-118, or possibly psalms 135 and 136, before departing for the Mount of Olives on the night of the Last Supper.[2] The entire collection is most appropriate for the hour of Evening Prayer.[3] The remaining selections are "easy" and popular psalms which most people can enter into with little difficulty.

In the canticle following the psalms the Church has restored to liturgical use beautiful hymns from the New Testament, some of which had their source in the early worship of the Christian communities while others very soon became part of ancient liturgical celebrations. These canticles, taken from Colossians, Ephesians, Philippians, 1 Peter, and Revelation, are distributed throughout the week. Every day we pray the Gospel canticle of Mary known as the "Magnificat." These beautiful canticles heighten the New Testament theme of Evening Prayer. They are brief and they are profound.

---

[1] John 13:1.

[2] See Matthew 26:17-30.

[3] Psalms 104-106 and 146-150 have also been known as Hallel psalms, but they are not assigned to Evening Prayer.

It is important to recognize and appreciate the rhythm of Evening Prayer which daily moves from the two psalms of the Old Testament to the two canticles of the New Testament. Some liturgy planners have succumbed to the fallacy, already commented on,[4] that two psalms and two canticles are too much prayer at one time. To justify brevity, an appeal is made to "Cathedral Vespers" as opposed to "Monastic Vespers." The monastic principle was to employ all 150 psalms, often in numerical order within a single week, without much attention to whether the psalms were appropriate to the time when they were offered, and frequently without much ceremony. The cathedral principle was to select psalms for their suitability to the evening hour, to heighten the celebration by symbols such as light and incense, to enrich the worship with chants and hymns, and to reflect the nature of the Church through diversity of ministries.[5] Brevity was not the goal. Our Liturgy of the Hours presents a happy modification of the monastic principle by distributing the psalms over a four week period and by arranging them, not numerically, but thematically. By any standard, Evening Prayer, even when sung, is not overlong or taxing.

The Magnificat

The New Testament theme reaches its climax in the Gospel canticle popularly known as the "Magnificat." This simple but splendid canticle is a mosaic of Old Testament texts which are realized in Mary and the Church, a meditation on the goodness of God and his saving deeds of loving kindness toward his people throughout history which reach their fullness in the person of Jesus Christ. From this meditation flows a joyful, even jubilant, spirit of praise and thanksgiving: "My soul proclaims the greatness of the Lord; my spirit rejoices in God my savior."

---

[4] See the first footnote of Chapter 7.

[5] See *The Liturgy of the Hours in East and West* by Robert Taft, S.J., The Liturgical Press, pages 32 and passim.

Luke places the words of this canticle on the lips of Mary not merely as an individual or even precisely as the mother of the Savior. In the full Lucan context, Mary is the personification of the Church and its model in prayer. Following the lead of St. Luke, the Vatican Council declared: "Mary is hailed as the preeminent and altogether singular member of the Church and as the Church's model and excellent exemplar in faith and charity."[6] Consequently as we pray this canticle we should realize that together with Mary we as members of the Church are the lowly servant whom God has lifted up. The Almighty has done great things for us, and has had mercy on us who fear him. And so we proclaim the greatness of the Lord and rejoice in God our Savior.[7]

Intercessory Prayers

The intercessory prayers of Vespers are different from those of Morning Prayer. The invocations at Morning Prayer consecrate or commend the day to God. The intercessions at Vespers are prayers for the benefit of the whole world. As such they are a generous kind of prayer and reflect an expansive spirit which reaches out in love and concern for everyone without exception. These intercessions are prayed in union with Jesus Christ who "opened his arms on the cross" to embrace all his people. They express the "catholic" aspect of Christian prayer and fulfill the exhortation of the Apostle: "I urge that petitions, prayers, intercessions and thanksgiving be offered for all, especially for kings and those in authority, that we may be able to lead undisturbed and tranquil lives in perfect piety and dignity. Prayer of this kind is good, and God our Savior is pleased with it, for he wants everyone to be saved and come to know the truth."[8] These petitions are similar to the Universal Prayer, or Prayer of the Faithful, at Mass.

---

[6] *Dogmatic Constitution on the Church*, 53.
[7] More comments on the Magnificat can be found in Chapter 14.
[8] 1 Timothy 2:1-4.

Spontaneous prayers are appropriate following the formulated intercessions, but such prayers should move from a limited concern to a more universal one. For example, a person may be mindful of a relative who is to be operated on; this prayer could possibly be phrased in this way: "For my brother who is to undergo surgery tomorrow and for all those who are seriously ill, we pray to you, Lord." These spontaneous petitions are expressed before the formulated intercession for the dead which, by tradition, is always the final petition.

The Spirit of Evening Prayer

The Eucharist should ordinarily be separated from Evening Prayer. If the Eucharist is celebrated before the dinner hour, evening prayer can easily follow dinner, or vice versa. It is not ideal to combine the two since they have different purposes. If Evening Prayer must be combined with the Eucharist, the intercessions from Evening Prayer may serve as the Prayer of the Faithful for Mass.

Evening Prayer sanctifies the closing hours of the day. It is the Church's way of living out the words of psalm 141: "Let my prayer arise before you like incense, the raising of my hands like an evening oblation." Although all the hours are ideally prayed in common, a special effort should be made to pray Vespers in common since this hour most clearly reflects in its New Testament theme the nature of the Church as the new people of God.

Evening Prayer with its New Testament theme invites us to focus on the person of Jesus as the Son who brings the Father's love to us and who offers our prayer to the Father. He does so by fulfilling his role as our priest, our mediator, our intercessor. Liturgical prayer is the prayer of Christ to his Father, and we do Christ proper honor by relating to him as our priest.

Arturo Toscanini was among the most renowned conductors of classical music in the twentieth century. One day during a pause in a particularly demanding but exhilarating rehearsal, the first violinist stood up and said in a loud voice, "Mr. Toscanini, I think you are the greatest conductor who ever lived." Toscanini stared at the man for a moment. He neither smiled nor frowned. Then in what was for him a soft voice, he said, "If you want to honor me, follow my conducting and play to the absolute best of your ability."

The great conductor of our liturgical worship, our high priest, is Jesus Christ. He not only directs us in our worship; he is actually present and active within us. Worship Christ we must since he is truly God, but in the celebration of the liturgy Christ in effect says to us: "If you want to honor me, follow my lead and worship the Father with me."

Christ is the Way, the Truth, and the Life. In the liturgy he shows us the way to the Father, he teaches us the truth of the Father, and he shares with us the life he has received from the Father. Catholic worship is trinitarian, not primarily in the sense that we honor the Father and the Son and the Holy Spirit, all in exactly the same way, but in the sense that we go to the Father in the power of the Holy Spirit who makes us one with Christ the Son. We ask the Father to grant our petitions "through our Lord Jesus Christ, your Son, who lives and reigns with you and the Holy Spirit, one God forever and ever." The priest concludes the Eucharistic Prayer, our offering of thanksgiving and praise, by elevating the body and the blood of the Lord in the holy sacrament and declaring to the Father: "Through him, with him, in him, in the unity of the Holy Spirit, all glory and honor is yours, almighty Father, forever and ever." Our resounding "Amen" is not only our affirmation of the Eucharistic Prayer but the recognition that Christ is our priest through, with, and in whom we adore, praise, and thank God the Father. The greatest honor we can give to Christ is to embrace him as our high priest and to be one with him in the worship of God the Father.

Each one of us should wish to join with our spiritual brothers and sisters in Christ to sing the praises of God who so loved the world that in the fullness of time he sent us his only-begotten Son.

CHAPTER TEN

Daytime Prayer

"Thy will be done." (Matthew 6:10)

WORKERS IN THE UNITED STATES ARE entitled by law to "coffee breaks" during the hours of their employment. The Church hopes that our devotion, and not a law, will lead us to take at least one "prayer break" during the day at a convenient time between Morning Prayer and Evening Prayer. Following the example of their Jewish ancestors and the apostolic Church, early Christians were accustomed to pray several times a day in the midst of their work. These varied times evolved monastically into the hours known as Terce (about 9:00 a.m.), Sext (about noon) and None (about 3:00 p.m.). The Second Vatican Council directed that those obliged to say the Office in choir were to continue to celebrate all three hours, but that one of the hours would be sufficient for everyone else. This reduction from the monastic practice is a recognition of the modern problem of living in a busy world, but the Church has retained one of these hours so that we may follow the ancient tradition of praying during the day while occupied with our work.

God's Will During the Day

"Daytime Prayer" is the name usually given now to the one hour retained by the Church from among the original three. Between 11:00

87

a.m. and 1:00 p.m. would seem to be about the ideal, but an earlier hour (approximating Terce) or a later hour (approximating None) is suitable.

The theme of this prayer is God's will. Its purpose is to recall to our minds that whatever our work may be, we are committed to following God's will by imitating Jesus who became obedient even to death on a cross (Philippians 2:8). This prayer reminds us of the Pauline exhortation, "Whatever you do, you should do all for the glory of God."[1] It also serves as a way of consecrating ourselves anew to the words we pray at Mass as well as at Morning and Evening Prayer, "Thy will be done." Since the Eucharist is our celebration of that obedience of Christ which won his exaltation from the Father,[2] Daytime Prayer has a special relationship to the Eucharist. It can look back to a morning Eucharist as a reaffirmation of our dedication to God's will as expressed in the Mass, or it can look forward to and prepare for an evening Eucharist.

Psalm 119 Sets the Theme

The theme of this prayer is set by the first psalm which is taken from psalm 119 (with the exception of Sundays, First Monday, and Third Friday; we will see why later). Psalm 119 is the longest psalm in the entire Psalter, running for 176 verses. It is divided by the acrostic method into sections of eight verses over the weekdays of four weeks. It has but one topic throughout: God's will. The psalmist mentions God's will in every one of the 176 verses without exception, but in order to avoid repeating the same word he uses many synonyms, such as commands, statutes, precepts, words, and promises. It is important to see that these expressions are indeed but synonyms for God's will lest we interpret the psalm in a legalistic sense. Notice the italicized words in the following section of the psalm as used on Tuesday of Week III:

---

[1] 1 Corinthians 10:31.
[2] Philippians 2:9.

Lord, how I love your *law*!
It is ever in my mind.

Your *command* makes me wiser than my foes;
for it is mine for ever.

I have more insight than all who teach me
for I ponder your *will*.

I have more understanding than the old
for I keep your *precepts*.

I turn my feet from evil paths
to obey your *word*.

I have not turned away from your *decrees*;
you yourself have taught me.

Your *promise* is sweeter to my taste
than honey in the mouth.

I gain understanding from your *precepts*;
I hate the ways of falsehood.

The second and third psalms are chosen from among those not used in the other hours, but more often than not they are suited to being prayed in an apostolic spirit. As apostolic prayers these psalms are eminently appropriate for Daytime Prayer.

Exceptions to Psalm 119

The first psalm of Daytime Prayer on Monday of Week I is not 119 but 19. Its theme is the same, God's will. On Friday of Week III, psalm 22 is used in three sections. It is the psalm placed on the lips of the dying Jesus by St. Matthew, "My God, my God, why have you forsaken me?"[3] It has been selected because of the relationship of every

---

[3] Matthew 27:46.

Friday to Good Friday. Sunday Daytime Prayer contains psalms suited to the celebration of the Lord's Day. First and Third Sundays employ psalm 118 in three parts. This psalm is a beautiful song of thanksgiving to God for his saving power. The New Testament sees this psalm as fulfilled in Christ.[4] The Church has incorporated verse 24 ("This day was made by the Lord; we rejoice and are glad") into its Easter celebration of which every Sunday is a reflection. Second and Fourth Sundays begin Daytime Prayer with psalm 23 (the Good Shepherd) and divide psalm 76 into two parts for the second and third psalms. Psalm 76 is a hymn of praise of God for his protecting presence among his people.

Readings and Prayer

Following the psalmody, Daytime Prayer presents a brief reading from Scripture. The purpose of this reading is to keep the Church's perspective that prayer is always dialogue: we speak to God and God speaks to us. The hour is concluded with a prayer which on weekdays and memorials is related directly to the time of day; on feasts and solemnities the prayer is proper.

A Practical Prayer

Daytime Prayer is very practical and even necessary in our busy world as it calls us back to a realization that all our occupations should be the carrying out of God's will. The fact that it is often difficult or troublesome to pray this hour is itself an indication of how vital the hour is to help us keep a prayerful realization of what we are about in our lives. The person who makes up his mind that this prayer is important will take the means to say it daily. When we find that we will be away from home at the time this prayer should be said, we can take the book

---

[4] Matthew 21:24 and Acts 4:11.

with us and make the opportunity to set aside the five minutes needed for a devout praying of this hour. A priest, for example, who is busy with visiting the sick and perhaps has an appointment at the chancery can sit in his car in a parking lot and say this prayer. A layman at work can set aside five minutes during his lunch break. Those living in community may find Daytime Prayer an appropriate way to begin or end a noon meal together. Where there is a will, there is indeed a way.

Union with Jesus and Mary

Daytime Prayer as emphasizing the will of God in our lives helps bring us into contact with two great moments in New Testament salvation history, its beginning and its climax. When the angel announced to Mary that she was to be the mother of Jesus, she responded to God's invitation by saying, "Be it done to me according to your word."[5] At that moment Jesus the Savior took flesh in the womb of Mary. St. Thomas Aquinas, following St. Luke's presentation of Mary as the personification of the Church, points out that Mary gave consent in the name of us all. This consent we can affirm in Daytime Prayer.

When Jesus was about to enter upon those final events of his salvific life, he struggled to accept the will of his Father. During his prayer in the garden, his plea was, "Father, if it is your will, take this cup from me." Then in a moment of supreme loving obedience, he cried out, "Yet not my will but yours be done."[6] "For the sake of the joy which lay before him he endured the cross, heedless of its shame."[7] "And it was thus that he humbled himself, obediently accepting even death, death on a cross! Because of this God highly exalted him and bestowed on him the name above every other name."[8] Daytime Prayer helps to unite us with Jesus in his prayer, "Not my will but yours be

---

[5] Luke 1:38.
[6] Luke 22:41.
[7] Hebrews 12:2.
[8] Philippians 2:8-9.

done," and directs us toward that moment of exaltation by the Father when we will be worthy of the name Christian.

The busier we are the more we need this simple but meaningful prayer given to us by the Church through the guidance of the Holy Spirit who helps us in our weakness to pray as we ought in order to make holy the day.

CHAPTER ELEVEN

The Office of Readings

"Speak, Lord, your servant is listening."
(1 Samuel 3:9)

THE OFFICE OF READINGS, FORMERLY known as Matins, has a long history with origins in the vigil service of the early Christians. Before the end of the first century it had become the practice for Christians to spend the entire night of Easter in prayer and meditation upon the Scriptures, waiting until the dawn of the resurrection. Later an abbreviated form of vigil preceded every Sunday as a little Easter. This night-time service with concentration on readings from Scripture was the forerunner of that part of the office which came to be known as Matins and is now the Office of Readings.

In the fourth century monasticism spread rapidly and the monks enthusiastically embraced the customary prayers of Christians as their supreme obligation. By the time of St. Benedict, who died around the year 543, this largely scriptural service had become a daily Office consisting of three divisions, called nocturnes, to be prayed through the night. Because of its length and the time of its celebration Matins became the office of monks to the exclusion of the laity and even the parochial clergy.

The Second Vatican Council wished to restore Matins to a form suitable for everyone. It directed that, for those obliged to recite the Office in choir, Matins should retain its nocturnal character and length, but that for others it should be shortened and adapted in such a way that it could be prayed at any hour of the day. As a result the Office of Readings now consists of three brief psalms and two readings. The first reading is biblical and the second is taken from the writings of the Fathers of the Church, or other authors, or from the lives of the saints. The biblical readings for the most part fill out what is missing from the readings assigned to the Mass so that virtually the entire Bible is covered by following both the Liturgy of the Hours and the Liturgy of the Eucharist.

The second reading is very enriching and broadening. Of special value are the selections from the ancient Fathers and some of the greatest theologian-saints of Christian history. The Fathers of the Church present the essentials of our faith in direct, strong language which is formative of the true Catholic spirit. I am particularly fond of Pope St. Leo the Great, St. John Chrysostom, and St. Gregory the Great, but many more contribute to the Office of Readings. It is like having a book called "The Best of the Fathers." In a whole lifetime I would never have read these selections if they had not been sifted out by the compilers from millions of words by the Fathers and conveniently presented to me in the breviary. Some of the theologian-saints I particularly benefit from are St. Thomas Aquinas, St. Charles Borromeo, and St. John Fisher, but there are more selections from St. Augustine than from any other writer.

The second reading on the feasts or memorials of the saints holds a special interest. This reading is frequently an excerpt from the writings of that saint, as for example on the memorial of St. Vincent de Paul on September 27 and that of St. Therese of Lisieux on October 1. It may be an observation by a saint about the saint of the day. Pope St. Gregory the Great tells a fascinating story about St. Scholastica, the sister of St. Benedict, on her memorial (February 10). On the memorial of Our Lady of Lourdes, February 11, it is intriguing to read a selection from a letter by St. Bernadette Soubirous in which she describes the vision she had of Mary. There are a few (not enough) selections from the documents of the Second Vatican Council, as well as from contemporary Popes; for example, the second reading for the memorial of the Ugandan martyrs on June 3 is from the homily of Pope Paul VI at the Mass of their canonization. Every day of the year the Office of Readings offers a splendid opportunity to grow in our faith.

In the Latin version of the Office of Readings there is a second set of biblical selections in a supplement; it is a two-year cycle of readings similar to the weekday cycle at Mass, but this supplement still awaits translation. The Catholic Book Publishing Company of New York in 1973 made available an excellent collection of both biblical and non-biblical readings in a two year cycle which is called simply *Christian Readings*.

Nature of the Office of Readings

The Office of Readings is unique among the liturgical hours, not only in that it is not related to a particular time of the day, but also in that it has its own orientation. Morning Prayer and Evening Prayer, Daytime Prayer and Night Prayer, all are primarily people speaking to God. Although in these hours the Church is very careful to maintain the dialogical aspect of prayer (man to God and God to man), listening is given little more than a nod. In the Office of Readings the reverse is true; therein the emphasis is on listening to God's word both in Scripture and in other sources. "Speak, Lord, your servant is listening" sums up the spirit of the Office of Readings. This emphasis tends to establish a balance in the entire Liturgy of the Hours between speaking and listening.

The purpose of the Office of Readings is different from that of the Liturgy of the Word in the Mass. The readings during Mass are not principally didactic. The Mass is a double communion with God, first in Word and then in Sacrament. The Liturgy of the Word forms one act of worship with the Liturgy of the Eucharist.[1] In the Office of Readings, especially on ferial days, the lessons are an end in themselves

---

[1] *Constitution on the Liturgy*, no. 56.

in the sense that they are not immediately directed toward some specific goal. We should come to the Office of Readings to hear the word of God, to ponder it at leisure and as deeply as possible. We should listen to God's word in a spirit of openness, eager to allow the word to form our thinking, to shape our lives, and to lead us wherever the Spirit wills. The Office of Readings, within the span of fifteen minutes or so, is meant to take on the character of a day of recollection or mini-retreat, the Holy Spirit himself being the retreat master.

Special Offices

The Office of Readings for Solemnities, Feasts, and most Memorials is of a different nature from that for ordinary weekdays. On these occasions the Office of Readings is thematic and usually carries the theme of the liturgical observance more completely than do the other hours. As such it forms an excellent preparation for a eucharistic celebration by enlightening us concerning the meaning of the liturgical observance and by forming within us the proper sentiments. It is still permissible to anticipate the Office of Readings after Vespers of the preceding day, and such anticipation before a Solemnity or Feast can be beneficial, especially if there is to be an early morning Eucharist. (For weekdays such anticipation seems to have no real value.) When the Eucharist is celebrated later in the day, anticipation is not necessary since the Office of Readings can easily be prayed before the Eucharist. On the other hand, some may prefer to have the Office of Readings after the Eucharist as a way of reflecting back upon its celebration and prolonging its spirit.

The special or "proper" Office of Readings helps to develop within us a spirituality which is formed by the liturgy of the Church in both its seasonal and sanctoral cycle. This is a solid spirituality, drawn not from merely human ideas or motives, but from the life of Jesus Christ and the example of the saints.

Other Uses

The Office of Readings can also be used to enhance days of recollection, retreats, and other devotions. On days other than Solemnities and Feasts it is quite correct to select psalms and readings in accord with some specific theme or purpose which would ordinarily be covered in a conference or sermon. A homily may follow the Readings as part of the Office. This arrangement has the advantage of placing a topic within the context of prayer. Devotions in honor of Mary or the saints can also be well served by being molded into the structure of an Office of Readings.

St. Augustine said that the Easter vigil is the mother of all vigils. That implies that there are "daughter" vigils, and such are still provided for in the Liturgy of the Hours. Those who wish to participate in a vigil for Sundays, Solemnities, and Feasts first celebrate the prescribed Office of Readings. They then add three canticles and a Gospel reading as indicated in Appendix I of the four volume set of the breviary. If a priest is present he may give a homily, or someone else may offer a reflection.

Reflective Listening

Since the emphasis in every form of the Office of Readings is on listening, rushing through it will accomplish little. This Office should be prayed at a time and in circumstances suitable for reflection. In common, a considerable period of time should be given to silence after the readings even before the responsories are made. The Church has been very careful to construct the Office of Readings in such a way that it may be prayed at any hour of the day precisely so that it may be prayed with an openness to hear the word of God.

"Pray that you may not be put to the test."
(Luke 22:40)

CHAPTER TWELVE

Night Prayer

"Into your hands I commend my spirit." (Psalm 31:6)

NIGHT PRAYER OR COMPLINE IS TO BE prayed as the last prayer of the day just before retiring, even after midnight if necessary. This prayer often becomes the favorite of many people, possibly because its symbolism is so clear. Darkness and sleep are biblically and poetically a symbol of death.

The poetic symbol is beautifully and simply painted by Robert Frost in his beloved poem, "Stopping by Woods on a Snowy Evening." Serenity pervades a quiet, peaceful, night:

> Whose woods these are I think I know.
> His home is in the village though;
> He will not see me stopping here
> To watch his woods fill up with snow,

Although he has no apparent reason to delay, the author seems almost compelled to pause in contemplation of the scene:

> My little horse must think it queer
> To stop without a farmhouse near
> Between the woods and frozen lake
> The darkest evening of the year.

> He gives his harness bells a shake
> To ask if there is some mistake.
> The only other sound's the sweep
> Of easy wind and downy flake.

There is a temptation to tarry but there is more to be done before a final surcease:

> The woods are lovely, dark and deep,
> But I have promises to keep,
> And miles to go before I sleep,
> And miles to go before I sleep.

Yes, miles to go before the sleep of slumber, and miles to go before the sleep of death.

Night Prayer prepares us not only for sleep but also for death. It is the Night Prayer of the day and of life itself.

The Paschal Mystery

Night Prayer centers on the paschal mystery, the heart of Christianity. We become Christian through baptism, our initial sharing in the paschal mystery, the death and resurrection of Christ. We celebrate this mystery in the Eucharist. We live it every day since a day is like a little lifetime. During each twenty-four hour period we live the paschal mystery in miniature: in sleep we die symbolically and in waking we come to life again. At a time chosen by God this cycle will end when we make the last passage through physical death to the fullness of life. In death we have our final sharing in the death of Christ and we look to the life-giving hand of the Father who will raise us to the glory of Christ's resurrection.

In the first Preface for Masses for the dead, the liturgy gives us a succinct expression of our faith: "In Christ who rose from the dead, our hope of resurrection dawned. The sadness of death gives way to the bright promise of immortality. Our life is changed, not ended. When the body of our earthly dwelling lies in death, we gain an everlasting dwelling place in heaven."

Elements of Night Prayer

Night Prayer is the time for an examination of conscience since symbolically we are about to appear before God in death. There should be a pause of some length to allow time for sincere reflection. (This is the "official" time for an examination of conscience; the pause at the beginning of Mass is for reflection on our unworthiness, an acknowledgment of sinfulness, but not an examination of conscience.) The silent examination leads to an expression of contrition and amendment.

The psalms of Night Prayer are of two kinds, prayers of trust and of lament. They are the sentiments of people who rely totally on God (the psalms of trust) or who through their human predicaments come to realize that in God alone can they place complete confidence (the psalms of lament). Trust and confidence are most appropriate themes for Night Prayer because there is something awesome and fearful about both sleep and death. For primitive people sleep meant that they exposed themselves to dangers from the elements, the animals, and their human enemies. In sleep they were defenseless, and there was no guarantee that they would wake to see the dawn. Perhaps the fear of primitive people is at least dimly reflected in little children who hate to go to bed. To some extent they don't want to miss anything, but within them there is a fear of darkness and sleep. As the parent turns out the light, a little child says, "I want a drink of water." He could have had a gallon of water before going to bed and he would still ask for a drink. He isn't thirsty. He is afraid. He is looking for some tactic which will keep his mother or father in the room a little longer.

When we grow to the sophistication of adulthood we lose our fear of sleep. And yet we have no guarantee that the "mechanism" which wakes us will work. Nor do we have any sure knowledge of what awaits us when we are carried in the arms of death through the dark door of mortality into the unknown. But we do have faith. We have faith that God waits to rouse us from death's slumber. We have confidence and trust that through death we will share in the life of the resurrected Christ. How appropriate for Night Prayer, then, are the psalms of confidence and trust.

"God Speaks" About Sleep

Charles Péguy, a French Catholic who died in 1914 during the First World War, composed a series of poems which are entitled *God Speaks*. The following are a few excerpts from a lengthy poem called "Sleep" in which God says:

> I don't like the man who doesn't sleep.
> Sleep is the friend of man.
> Sleep is the friend of God.
> Sleep is perhaps the most beautiful thing I have created.
>
> He whose heart is pure, sleeps.
> And he who sleeps has a pure heart.
>
> But they tell me that there are men
> Who work well and sleep badly.
> Who don't sleep. What a lack of confidence in me.
>
> They look after their business very well during the day,
> But they haven't enough confidence in me
> To let me look after it during one night.
>
> Human wisdom says:
> Woe to the man who puts off what he has to do until
> tomorrow. And I say
> Blessed, blessed is the man who puts off what he has to
> do until tomorrow.

Blessed is he who puts off. That is to say Blessed is he
who hopes. And who sleeps.

Péguy wrote this poem for himself as he struggled in the face of
tragedies to trust in God. I have no idea whether he ever prayed the
psalms of Night Prayer, but he would have loved them. Their expression of trust led Pope John XXIII, the story goes, to say at night, "It is
your Church, Lord. I am going to bed." Whether the Pope actually said
that or not, it is the right disposition for night prayer.

The theme of confidence and trust reaches a climax in the
responsory to the Scripture reading: "Into your hands, Lord, I commend my spirit." These words of psalm 31 St. Luke placed on the lips
of the dying Savior (Luke 23:46). Through these same words we can
effectively unite our death with that of Christ. And because of our union
with him, we can say with complete confidence, "You have redeemed
us, Lord God of truth." In the Gospel canticle of Simeon, which follows
the responsory, we identify with an old man who is about to die, a man
who approaches death willingly because he has seen salvation in the
person of Jesus Christ. Simeon was overjoyed to take the Christ Child
into his arms, to feel the tiny heart beating close to his own, to feel the
warmth of life radiating from the little body. We are more blessed than
Simeon. We are privileged to receive the body and the blood of the
risen Savior, the pledge of everlasting life. In faith we hear the consoling
promise of Christ: "You who eat my flesh and drink my blood have life
everlasting and I will raise you up on the last day." The sacramental
meaning of the Eucharist is the foundation of the symbolism of Night
Prayer and its power makes that symbolism real.

Dying and Rising with Christ

By a long tradition dating back at least to St. Benedict, who died
around the year 543, Evening Prayer concluded with a hymn to our
Lady. This hymn has now been placed after Night Prayer. Several
choices are available, two of which have explicit allusions to death. In

the "Hail, Holy Queen," we say: "After this our exile show us the
blessed fruit of your womb, Jesus," and in the "Hail Mary" we say:
"Pray for us sinners now and at the hour of our death." But in any of
the hymns to our Lady we honor the glorified mother of the Savior,
God's highly favored daughter who in her assumption has already
shared in the resurrection of her Son. Mary, the model of the Church,
taken body and soul to heaven, is a sign that we as members of the
Church will pass through death to a sharing in the resurrection of
Christ.

Importance of this Hour

Our weariness at the end of the day can make Night Prayer a
chore. It is so easy simply to fall into bed without a further thought that
we may be tempted to forget all about still another prayer. But our
fatigue itself should remind us that we are frail, that every moment
brings us closer to the ultimate moment of death. We need to place
ourselves in the hands of our loving Father before we close our eyes in
sleep just as we hope to be received by our Father when we close our
eyes in death.

Night Prayer sanctifies the final hour of the day. But it does more.
It sanctifies our entire lives since the heart of our lives is the paschal
mystery. Dying is the most important act of living. It is the final
expression of faith in God the Father as life-giver. As such death should
be embraced willingly, and in the sentiments of Night Prayer we make
our death voluntary in union with that of Christ. We may think that we
have miles to go before we sleep, but each day those miles become
fewer in number. Truly this prayer is the night prayer of the day and
of life itself.

Part III

MORE PSALMS,
THE CANTICLES OF EVENING
AND MORNING PRAYER,
AND DIRECTIVES

"Christ continues his priestly work through the agency of his
Church, which is ceaselessly engaged in praising the Lord and
interceding for the salvation of the whole world."

(Constitution on the Liturgy, no. 83)

"In his anguish Jesus prayed with great intensity, and his sweat became like drops of blood falling to the ground." (Luke 22:44)

CHAPTER THIRTEEN

More Psalms, Some Comments

"All raised their voice in prayer to God." (Acts 4:24)

SISTER CORITA KENT, I.H.M. DURING a lecture on art displayed one of her abstract paintings. Someone from the audience asked her, "What does that painting mean?" "What does it mean?" Sister repeated, as if puzzled by the question. "It means whatever you want it to mean."

The psalms do not mean whatever we want them to mean since they are the work of the Holy Spirit through designated human authors, and yet we do understand them and pray them in the light of fuller revelation. Our interpretation, even a prayerful one, is judged by the analogy of faith, that is, by comparison with other clear statements of doctrine. Psalm 16 provides a good example. It was composed at a time when belief in life after death was very vague at best. The psalmist says to the Lord:

> You will show me the path of life,
> the fullness of joy in your presence,
> at your right hand happiness forever.

"The path of life" referred to the way to holiness. "Happiness forever" was understood to mean the span of life on this earth. And yet we are quite correct hermeneutically to profess in these words our faith in everlasting life with the Lord in heaven. The interpretations of the following psalms are in accord, I believe, with the analogy of faith and are proper ways to offer them as the prayer of Christians.

Although the psalms are centered on the God of Israel who is the Father of our Lord Jesus Christ, the royal psalms help us to focus on the person of Christ, the Son of God the Father. Three royal psalms are of particular interest: 20, 21, and 110.

Psalm 20, Tuesday Evening Prayer, Week I

This royal psalm is a prayer for the king's victory. In the first half the people in the Temple pray that the sacrifice the king himself will offer to the Lord may be acceptable. This sentiment is clear in the following verses selected from the first three stanzas of the psalm:

> May the Lord remember all your offerings
> and receive your sacrifice with favor.
> May the Lord grant all your prayers.

Then the king offers his sacrifice. Following the offering the people express their confidence:

> I am sure now that the Lord
> will give victory to his anointed,
> and will reply from his holy heaven
> with the mighty victory of his hand.

When praying in common, it is helpful to pause after the third stanza to allow time for a reflection on the sacrifice of Christ. In fact, the first three stanzas are an excellent introduction to Mass or could be chanted as an opening hymn. The final three stanzas are an appropriate prayer after communion.

Psalm 21, Tuesday Evening Prayer, Week I

This royal psalm reflects the relationship between the Lord and the King, and was part of a liturgy of thanksgiving as the following selected verses indicate:

> O Lord, your strength gives joy to the king.
> He asked you for life and this you have given,
> days that will last from age to age.

I personally find this psalm a heart-warming meditation on Jesus and his Father, the love between them, and the complete dedication of God to his beloved:

> You have granted your blessings to him forever.
> You have made him rejoice with the joy of your
> presence.

I am moved to join enthusiastically in the conclusion:

> O Lord, we shall sing and praise your power.

Psalm 110, Sunday Evening Prayer

This royal psalm is a favorite for Evening Prayer. In fact, it is used on all four Sundays of the month, as well as on Solemnities and many feast days. It is a royal psalm which we apply to Christ the King, as does the New Testament.[1] The shifts within its structure may strike us as strange. It begins with an oracle about the eminent place of the master, the king (Christ): "The Lord's revelation to my Master: `Sit on my right: your foes I will put beneath your feet.'" Then it addresses the King:

> The Lord will wield from Zion
> your scepter of power:
> rule in the midst of all your foes.

---

[1] See Acts 2:34-35, Hebrews 1:5, and Matthew 22:42-46.

Next God himself speaks:

> A prince from the day of your birth
> on the holy mountains;
> from the womb before the dawn I begot you.

God's proclamation suggests the extraordinary nature of the birth of the prince who was to become king. The Hebrew text of this verse is not clear; another translation is possible:

> Yours is princely power in the day of your birth
> in holy splendor; before the day star,
> like the dew I have begotten you.

This translation from the *New American Bible* conveys more of the mysterious quality of the birth. The prince is begotten even before the sun was created, conceived like the dew which appears in the morning (without explanation as far as the ancients were concerned).

This king-to-be, born in such an extraordinary manner, will also have an extraordinary ministry, not only as king, but as a priest, not as a levitical priest by birth, but as a unique priest in the order of Melchizedek.[2] In Israel a king sometimes performed the functions of a priest, and a prophet could have been born a levitical priest, as was Jeremiah, but it was unheard of that one person would be all three: prophet, king, and priest.

The meaning of the final verse is obscure. It may suggest that despite his extraordinary origin and the divine assistance afforded him, the king suffers weariness in his humanity, but after refreshment he continues in his mission:

> He shall drink from the stream by the wayside
> and therefore he shall lift up his head.

The translation by the International Committee on English in the Liturgy renders the final verse as follows:

---

[2] See Genesis 14:18 and the commentary on this passage in Chapter 7 of the Epistle to the Hebrews.

> The victor drinks
> from a wayside stream
> and rises refreshed.

Because of our faith in Christ, we readily see him in this psalm. He sits at the right hand of the Father in heaven. He has a mysterious birth in eternity from the Father, he is given an extraordinary birth in time from a virgin. He is indeed both king and priest, as well as prophet. In his humanity he suffers for us but he lifts up his head in the glory of his resurrection. This royal psalm becomes a wisdom psalm for us when through it we reflect on the mystery of Christ.

Psalm 24, Tuesday Morning Prayer, Week I

This psalm seems to have accompanied a procession to the Temple. The original setting is not certain, but the procession may have been the return of a king from a victorious battle. During the procession a choir of the people chants phrases indicating the conduct which makes people worthy to enter the Temple of the Lord:

> Who shall climb the mountain of the Lord?
> The one with clean hands and pure heart,
> who desires not worthless things,
> who has not sworn so as to deceive his neighbor.

During the procession it may have been that the priests were carrying the Ark of the Covenant, which represented the presence of God. As the king and his retinue approach the gates of the city they cry out:

> O gates, lift high your heads;
> grow higher, ancient doors.
> Let him enter, the king of glory!

Some people from within, who personify the gates, demand to know the identity of the one who wants to enter:

> Who is the king of glory?

Those in the procession answer the question and repeat their demand:

> The Lord, the mighty, the valiant,
> The Lord, the valiant in war.
> O gates, lift high your heads:
> grow higher, ancient doors.
> Let him enter, the king of glory!

But again those inside demand to know who enters:

> Who is he, the king of glory?

The final, insistent response is:

> He, the Lord of armies,
> he is the king of glory.

This psalm can be dramatized to accompany a procession of the Blessed Sacrament or of the Bible. I see in it a spiritual significance, a preparation for holy communion: the need to open wide our hearts to receive the Lord.

Psalm 43, Tuesday Morning Prayer, Week II

This psalm originally formed a single prayer with psalm 42 which is part of Morning Prayer on Monday of Week II. It is the lament of a person who far from Jerusalem yearns to be part of the Temple worship. Psalm 43 was part of the prayers at the foot of the altar in the missal of Pope Pius V (1570) which was in use until the Second Vatican Council. The psalm was chosen because of the following verses:

> O send forth your light and your truth;
> let these be my guide.

> Let them bring me to your holy mountain
> to the place where you dwell.
> And I will come to the altar of God,
> the God of my joy.

I like to pray this psalm in the person of those who, for whatever reason, are separated from the Church and the Eucharist, but I also find within it a cause for thanksgiving that the Eucharist is readily available to us. We no longer need to go to the Temple as to the only place where sacrifice is offered. In fact, wherever Christ gathers priest and people, there the Eucharist may be celebrated.

Psalm 55, Wednesday Daytime Prayer of Week II

One reason to include Daytime Prayer as a regular part of our piety is that otherwise we miss out on some remarkable psalms. One of these is psalm 55, the lament of a person who has been betrayed by a close friend. I can offer this prayer in an apostolic spirit in the person of those who suffer the pain of the psalmist today, but no one who has read the Gospel account of the betrayal by Judas can fail to see Jesus in the following poignant verses of psalm 55:

> If this had been done by an enemy
> I could bear his taunts.
> If a rival had risen against me,
> I could hide from him.
> But it is you, my own companion,
> my intimate friend!
> How close was the friendship between us.
> We walked together in harmony
> in the house of God.

This psalm draws me close to Jesus in his hour of deep sorrow.

Psalm 139, Wednesday Evening Prayer of Week IV

Not all the verses of this psalm are included in the version for the Liturgy of the Hours. The selected verses (1-18 and 23-24) can be considered a psalm of praise and thanksgiving. It worships God who enfolds us in his loving arms even when we make the mistake of trying to twist free like a discontented child. When people discover this lovely prayer, it often becomes one of their favorites. Very beautiful is the following sentiment:

> It was you who created my being,
> knit me together in my mother's womb.
> I thank you for the wonder of my being,
> for the wonders of all your creation.

This text should not be taken as a proof that the fetus is alive and human (such, after all, is a scientific fact which does not need proof, only acceptance), but it does urge us to pray in the person of unborn children.

Psalm 51, Friday Morning Prayer

This psalm of lament, a penitential prayer, has been assigned to Morning Prayer on the Fridays of all four weeks. The psalm admits sinfulness frankly and begs earnestly for mercy and forgiveness. The author sees that forgiveness must be complemented by renewed piety, and so there is a petition that a sinful spirit may be replaced by purity of life:

> From my sins turn away your face
> and blot out all my guilt.
> A pure heart create in me, O God,
> put a steadfast spirit within me.

This prayer is very appropriate for that day on which Christ, the

Lamb of God, died to take away the sins of the world. It has been such a favorite that some religious used to have the practice of memorizing it so that it could be recited silently while going to and coming from the chapel or the dining room.

Confidence in Praying the Psalms

To give a commentary on all one hundred and fifty psalms is beyond the scope of this book, nor is such necessary for the purpose of fostering prayer. We should have confidence that we can pray the psalms authentically and devoutly without an elaborate study of their exegesis. This is not to support literalism but to recognize that the psalms, although composed centuries ago within a culture far removed from our own, have succeeded in being the prayer of every generation of Christians from the time the Church was born from the pierced side of Christ as he lay dying on the cross. The reason for this success is that the Spirit has come upon the people of the Church in every age, the same Spirit who is the ultimate author of the psalms. The Holy Spirit guides and inspires us during our prayer.

Catholics of an earlier era were given the impression that they must be very careful about reading the Bible lest they fall into a false interpretation, and that impression scared many of them away. We should not have that fear about the psalms. They are God's gift to us to help us pray as we ought. On the other hand, we should value the psalms so much that we are eager to study and learn more about them. I have never read a book, studied a commentary, or listened to a lecture on the topic of the psalms without gaining a better knowledge and a deeper devotion. It is helpful to read the psalms in various translations. That often yields helpful insights which are not possible from a single translation.

Praying the psalms should be a lifelong experience, and their study should be a lifelong endeavor. All the effort is worth it so that in union with Christ we may come together in prayer.

"This is how you are to pray: 'Our Father in heaven. . .'"
(Matthew 6:9)

CHAPTER FOURTEEN

The Canticles of Evening Prayer

"Your attitude must be that of Christ." (Philippians 2:5)

CANTICLES FROM THE NEW TESTAMENT happily endow Evening Prayer with hymns that reflect the blessings which have come to us in Christ Jesus. The fullness of the day when Evening Prayer is offered symbolizes the fullness of revelation in Christ for which we offer thanks and praise to God.

Evening Prayer I of Sunday (Philippians 2:5-11)

The liturgical week begins with Evening Prayer on Saturday, which is designated as Evening Prayer I of Sunday. It is also known as First Vespers of Sunday. The New Testament canticle is from Philippians 2:5-11 which not only proclaims the meaning of the incarnation and the paschal mystery, but also stirs us to join Christ throughout all of our prayers in his worship of his Father.

The translation currently approved for the Liturgy of the Hours in the United States is as follows:

> Though he was in the form of God,
> Jesus did not deem equality with God
> something to be grasped at.

117

Rather, he emptied himself
and took the form of a slave,
being born in the likeness of men.

He was known to be of human estate,
and it was thus that he humbled himself,
obediently accepting even death,
death on a cross!

Because of this,
God highly exalted him
and bestowed on him the name
above every other name,

So that at Jesus' name
every knee must bend
in the heavens, on the earth,
and under the earth,
and every tongue proclaim
to the glory of God the Father:
JESUS CHRIST IS LORD!

This canticle shows that Jesus became human for the sake of the cross, that the incarnation leads to the paschal mystery of his death and resurrection, and that everything which Jesus did was for the glory of his Father. The passage invites us to see that resurrection did not follow the death of Jesus as subsequent in time, but that the resurrection was the direct result of his obedient embracing of the cross. It would be appropriate to add emphasis by means of capital letters: "He humbled himself, obediently accepting even death, death on a cross! BECAUSE of this God highly exalted him. . . ."

In the conclusion of the hymn, the translator has unfortunately given an inappropriate emphasis by the use of capitals and has inverted the original Greek text. The final three verses should read:

and every tongue proclaim

that Jesus Christ is Lord
TO THE GLORY OF GOD THE FATHER.

The Greek text places the phrase, "to the glory of God the Father" in the climactic position. This placement is significant because the hymn is preceded by an exhortation from St. Paul: "Your attitude must be that of Christ," or as another rendition has it, "Have this mind in you which was also in Christ Jesus." That attitude, that mind of Christ, is loving obedience for the glory of God the Father. This example of Christ directs us to offer liturgical prayer through Christ to the Father. During Lent we offer a petition: "Jesus, our Christ, you promised to be with those who pray in your name — help us always to pray with you to the Father in the Holy Spirit."[1] That is the shape of liturgical prayer, and every Saturday evening we have a reminder that liturgical prayer in accord with the mind of Christ is not the prayer to Christ, but the prayer of Christ to his Father.

Evening Prayer II of Sunday (Revelation 19:1-7)

The canticle for Evening Prayer II (also known as Second Vespers) of Sunday is a jubilant hymn of praise to which the liturgy has added multiple "Alleluias." The source is the Book of Revelation 19:1-7. John writes, "I heard what sounded like the loud song of a great assembly in heaven." This is how the song begins:

> Alleluia.
> Salvation, glory and power to our God.
> Alleluia.
> His judgments are honest and true.
> Alleluia.

It is the great wedding feast of the Lamb of God in heaven. The liturgical excerpt concludes as follows:

---

[1] Evening Prayer for Tuesday of the Fifth Week of Lent.

> The wedding feast of the lamb has begun
> and his bride is prepared to welcome him.
> Alleluia.

I personally wish that the liturgical excerpt had continued through to verse 9. Then the conclusion would read:

> She has been given a dress to wear
> made of finest linen, brilliant white,
> the virtuous deeds of God's saints.
> Happy are they who have been invited
> to the wedding feast of the lamb.

The final verse is the source of the words of the priest at Mass just before communion: "This is the Lamb of God who takes away the sins of the world. Happy are those who are called to his supper." The supper is not the Last Supper, as some suppose, or even the supper of the Eucharist at that moment, but the supper in which the Eucharist will be fulfilled, the eternal banquet in heaven. I trust that no one will hesitate to add these two verses to the hymn either in private recitation or communal celebration.

During Lent the Sunday canticle is taken from a passage in the First Letter of Peter which reflects on the sufferings of Christ.[2]

Monday Evening Prayer (Ephesians 1:3-10)

The canticle for Monday is a magnificent passage drawn from the first chapter of the Letter to the Ephesians. Scholars agree the text is almost certainly from an early liturgical hymn. There are three stanzas. The first emphasizes the Father, the second the Son, and the third the Holy Spirit. God the Father is the source of every spiritual blessing which comes to us in Christ when we are sealed by the Holy Spirit, and

---

[2] 1 Peter 2:21-24.

all is done for the praise of the Father's glory. The passage is not only a beautiful hymn but a doctrinal instruction on the proper trinitarian orientation which should shape our spirituality and our prayer. The liturgical selection in the breviary, however, is limited to eight verses and skips a phrase. That does not do justice to the passage.

Particularly unfortunate is the fact that the verses concerning the Holy Spirit are omitted. It is very worthwhile to read and to ponder the entire section which begins with the third verse and concludes with the fourteenth. One can hope that in a future edition of the Liturgy of the Hours the entire passage will be included at Evening Prayer on Mondays.

Tuesday Evening Prayer (Revelation 4:11; 5:9, 10, 12)

The canticle of Tuesday Evening Prayer lifts us to the heavenly court where God the Father is worshipped on his throne:

> O Lord our God, you are worthy
> to receive glory and honor and power.
> For you have created all things;
> by your will they came to be and were made.

Then attention is turned to God the Son, the Lamb of God:

> Worthy are you, O Lord,
> to receive the scroll and break open its seals.

The scroll records the plan of God for our salvation which is accomplished by means of the paschal mystery of the death and resurrection of the Lamb:

> For you were slain;
> with your blood you purchased for God
> men of every race and tongue,
> of every people and nation.

In baptism we have been consecrated as a priestly people, destined to join the Lamb in worship of the Father:

> You made of them a kingdom
> and priests to serve our God
> and they shall reign on the earth.

We conclude with a beautiful acknowledgment of Christ as the sacrificial lamb:

> Worthy is the Lamb that was slain
> to receive power and riches,
> wisdom and strength,
> honor and glory and praise.

This short but striking canticle with its heavenly vision reminds us of our eternal destiny.

Wednesday Evening Prayer (Colossians 1:12-20)

The Letter to the Colossians emphasizes the pre-eminence of Christ and his superiority over all creation. From the first chapter the Liturgy of the Hours has selected a passage which, some scholars maintain, was adapted from a Christian hymn. The passage begins, in accord with New Testament revelation, with an acknowledgment of God the Father:

> Let us give thanks to the Father
> for having made you worthy
> to share the lot of the saints
> in light.
> He rescued us
> from the power of darkness
> and brought us
> into the kingdom of his beloved Son.

The mention of the kingdom provides a smooth transition to the praise of Christ:

> He is the image of the invisible God,
> the first-born of all creatures.
> In him everything in heaven and on earth
> was created,
> things visible and invisible.

From the theme of creation we move to that of redemption through the blood of the cross. Christ is also hailed as "the head of the body, the Church." As head, we are here reminded, Christ draws us to himself as the members of his body. It is this truth which makes real our apostolic prayer in the person of those who come under Christ's headship.

Thursday Evening Prayer (Revelation 11:17-18; 12:10b-12a)

On Thursday evening we return to the Book of Revelation for our canticle. The scene is heaven where loud voices proclaim: "The kingdom of the world now belongs to our Lord and his Anointed and he will reign forever and ever." This proclamation serves as an introduction to the hymn of praise which begins:

> We praise you, the Lord God Almighty
> who is and who was.
> You have assumed your great power,
> you have begun your reign.

The canticle then goes on to recount God's great saving work through his Son, the Anointed.

Friday Evening Prayer (Revelation 15:3-4)

Friday too selects a canticle from the Book of Revelation. It is a great victory song in honor of our all powerful God. It begins:

> Mighty and wonderful are your works,
> Lord God Almighty!
> Righteous and true are your ways,
> O King of the nations!

The context informs us that this is both the song of Moses, the servant of God, and the song of the Lamb. That means that God is praised both for the deliverance of the Israelites from the slavery of sin and for our salvation in Christ. We are reminded that the God of Israel is the God of Christians.

The Magnificat of Mary (Luke 1:46-55)

In every Evening Prayer we offer Mary's canticle which is known by its first word in Latin, "Magnificat." The canticle comes from that episode in the Gospel of St. Luke which we call the Visitation,[3] when Mary went to help her relative, Elizabeth, who was pregnant with John the Baptist. When Mary arrived, Elizabeth was inspired to recognize her as the most favored of all women because of the child she was bearing whose identity was revealed to Elizabeth. She cried out in words which have become very familiar to us: "Blessed are you among women and blessed is the fruit of your womb."

Mary's response to this greeting gives us our canticle for Evening Prayer. This prayer manifests Mary's humility according to which she praised God because of his special favor toward the lowly and the poor, of whom Mary counted herself a part. Mary's words seem to be almost a corrective of the praise offered to her by Elizabeth. It is as if Mary were

---

[3] Luke 1:39-56.

saying, "Don't give me the glory. Give the glory to God, as I do, because he has done great things for me": "My soul proclaims the greatness of the Lord, my spirit rejoices in God my savior, for he has looked with favor on his lowly servant."

We offer this prayer in union with Mary because she is our model as members of the Church. We are the lowly servants whom God has lifted up with his resurrected Son. The Almighty has done great things for us and has had mercy on us. We proclaim the greatness of the Lord and rejoice in God our Savior.

Although Mary's canticle is from the New Testament, it is an echo of Old Testament sentiments, particularly the prayer of Hannah, the mother of the prophet Samuel.[4] As a Jewish girl Mary was familiar with these sentiments. They recall our Old Testament roots and become a transition to New Testament fulfillment.

---

[4] I Samuel 2:1-10. Hannah's canticle is part of Morning Prayer for Wednesdays of Week II.

"If you with all your sins know how to give your children good things, how much more will the heavenly Father give the Holy Spirit to those who ask him."
(Luke 11:13)

CHAPTER FIFTEEN

The Canticles of Morning Prayer

"Servants of the Lord, bless the Lord." (Daniel 3:85)

RENOWNED THOUGH THE ONE HUNDRED and fifty psalms are, they are not the only prayerful expressions found throughout the pages of the Old Testament. From the many biblical prayers outside the Book of Psalms, the liturgy has selected twenty-six to be part of Morning Prayer.

You probably will not want to read this chapter through in one sitting. Give it a try, but you may prefer to consult it when, as you are praying Morning Prayer, you discover that you would like some background and comments on one or more of the canticles.

Sunday of Week I (Daniel 3:57-88, 56)

From the third chapter of the Book of Daniel the liturgy has selected a canticle which is used twice in the month, on the first and third Sundays. The book is of late origin, having been composed during the terrible persecution carried on by Antiochus IV Epiphanes (167-164 B.C.) in order to comfort the people and to strengthen their faith. The third chapter tells the story of three young Jews who survived by the favor of God when they were thrown into a fiery furnace by a sinister king. The canticle is their hymn of thanksgiving and praise. During prayer in common it may be offered in litany style, the leader, for example, saying "Angels of the Lord," and the community responding "Bless the Lord," and so through the entire canticle. (Another example of litany style is psalm 136 at Evening Prayer on Monday of Week IV, the refrain being "for his love endures forever.")

Monday of Week I (1 Chronicles 9:10b-13)

King David had an earnest desire to build a Temple to the glory of God. This project fell to his son, Solomon, but before David died he asked the people to donate what they could for the construction of the Temple. He asked, "Who is willing to contribute generously to the Lord?" The people responded so lavishly that David was delighted and offered a canticle of praise and thanks to God. This is a short, simple prayer which can be offered without any reference to its context, but when praying it I like to be mindful of the people who make contributions to the Church, especially those who like the widow in the Gospel are generous with whatever they have.

Tuesday of Week I (Tobit 13:1b-8)

If you have never read the entire Book of Tobit, you can give yourself a treat. It is like a short novel which was composed to teach Jewish morality and piety. Although it was written in the second century B.C., it tells the story of Tobit and his family who lived among the captives deported to Nineveh in 721 B.C. This canticle is Tobit's joyful song of praise to God for his providential care. Living as we do in a kind of exile within a society whose values are foreign to those of the Gospel, we can readily make this prayer our own.

Wednesday of Week I (Judith 16:1, 13-15)

The Book of Judith was composed near the end of the second century B.C. It teaches how God used Judith (whose name means "Jewess") as his instrument in defeating Holofernes, an Assyrian general. The narrative becomes rather gory, but fortunately we can pray Judith's canticle of thanksgiving for victory without any reference to its military context. The canticle in the Bible is introduced this way: "Judith led all Israel in this song of thanksgiving, and the people swelled this hymn of praise." We are led by Christ and we do well to offer this jubilant canticle enthusiastically with him in thanksgiving for his victory over sin and death.

Thursday of Week I (Jeremiah 31:10-14)

Jeremiah was born a priest and he was called to be a prophet. His contemporaries thought of him as a prophet of doom since he warned them that their return to old idolatries would seal their fate as victims of the powerful Babylonian army of Nebuchadnezzar. Because of his sufferings, his imprisonment, and his public disgrace, Jeremiah is seen as a Christ figure. After the people were carried off into exile, Jeremiah promised the restoration of the nation in a section of the biblical presentation which is called the Book of Consolation. It is from this section that this canticle in the Liturgy of the Hours is taken.

Friday of Week I (Isaiah 45:15-25)

The second part of Isaiah, which contains this canticle, was composed during the exile in Babylon which Jeremiah had foretold. The people lived in the midst of an idolatrous society, among whom the Lord, unlike the idols, seemed to be hidden. This canticle is an assurance of both faith and hope which speaks to us today, living as we do in a snobbish society which is dedicated to the idols of power, prestige, and wealth.

Saturday of Week I (Exodus 15:1-4a, 8-13, 17-18)

This canticle is a hymn of victory after the crossing of the Red Sea. The exodus was the great saving event of Israel as the paschal mystery of the death and resurrection of Christ is for us. We can offer this prayer both in union with our ancestors in faith as well as in union with the people God has made his own in Christ.

Sunday of Week II (Daniel 3:52-57)

This canticle is a song to the Lord by Azariah from the midst of the fire into which he and his companions had been thrust by the king. See the comments on Sunday of Week I, but this canticle can stand on its own without any reference to its context.

Monday of Week II (Sirach 36:1-5, 10-13)

The Book of Sirach was composed around the year 180 B.C. and is part of the wisdom literature of the Bible. It has also been called "Ecclesiasticus" or "Church Book" because of the extensive use the Church has made of this book in presenting moral teaching. This prayer follows upon the author's teaching that "He who serves God willingly is heard; his petition reaches the heavens. The prayer of the lowly pierces the clouds; it does not rest until it reaches its goal" (35:16-17).

Tuesday of Week II (Isaiah 38:10-14, 17b-20)

When King Hezekiah fell mortally ill, the prophet Isaiah came to him and warned him "to put his house in order" because he was about to die. The King wept tears of sorrow and entreated the Lord to spare him. God heard his prayer and granted him fifteen more years of life. This canticle is his prayer of thanksgiving.

Wednesday of Week II (1 Samuel 2:1-10)

Hannah was barren until the Lord answered her earnest prayer. She conceived Samuel, whom she dedicated to the Lord in accord with a promise she had made to God. Her son became a great prophet. This canticle is her hymn of thanksgiving to God, who gave her a son despite her previous sterility. In its praise of God who favors the poor and lifts up the lowly it foreshadows the Magnificat of Mary who conceived Jesus while remaining a virgin.

Thursday of Week II (Isaiah 12:1-6)

Isaiah prophesied the reign of Immanuel, the offspring of David. He promised that God would gather together the outcasts of Judah, that the north and the south would be united, and that on that day the people would praise and thank the Lord in the words of this canticle. Christ fulfills this prophecy by gathering people of every race and nation into the Church, and in union with him we offer this canticle of thanksgiving.

Friday of Week II (Habakkuk 3:2-4, 13a, 15-19)

Habakkuk lived during a time when widespread political intrigue and the practice of idolatry seemed to make punishment from God inevitable. In fact, God warned that Babylon would be his chastising rod. After a dialogue with God in which he challenged God about the manner in which he governed the world, Habakkuk acquiesced and offered a prayer which is a remarkable act of faith and a pledge to persevere in dedication to God, no matter what might come. That prayer is our canticle on Friday of Week II. A seminarian once told me that he has made this prayer his own in order to pledge to God his resolution to persevere faithfully in priestly ministry, no matter what may come. I pray this canticle not only for myself but in union with all those who earnestly desire to remain faithful to God in their calling.

Saturday of Week II (Deuteronomy 32:1-12)

For centuries before the Book of Deuteronomy was composed, Israel had pondered the significance of the exodus and its consequences, that mighty act of God on their behalf. Deuteronomy is a re-telling of the events in the plain of Moab between the wanderings in the desert and the crossing of the Jordan. The canticle for this Saturday is proclaimed in the person of Moses. We should realize that the saving act of God in the passover and exodus is actually one great providential movement which reaches its climax in Christ's paschal mystery of his death and resurrection.

Sunday of Week III (Daniel 3:57-88, 56)

See the comments for Sunday of Week I.

Monday of Week III (Isaiah 2:2-5)

This canticle is a vision of the messianic future when Mount Zion will be sacred to all peoples. The Israelites were not told to be proselytizers but they were expected to attract people to Jerusalem by the sincerity of their worship, a lesson for us as well. The promise which is strikingly expressed in the poetic phrase about beating swords into plowshares is a work for us still to accomplish.

Tuesday of Week III (Isaiah 26:1b-4, 7-9, 12)

This canticle is modeled on the psalms of trust. It is within the context of a belief that a remnant will remain after devastation and a hope that salvation will come by the power of God. As always with Isaiah, the poetry is beautiful and the theology profound.

Wednesday of Week III (Isaiah 33:13-16)

The context of this canticle is a long prophecy about a powerful enemy, the ultimate defeat of that enemy, and the restoration of Jerusalem. It begins in the voice of God: "Hear, you who are far off, what I have done." Echoes of the first psalm can be heard in its theology of the victory of the just and the defeat of the wicked.

Thursday of Week III (Isaiah 40:10-17)

This canticle comes from the second part of Isaiah (Deutero-Isaiah) which was composed by a disciple of the great prophet toward the end of the Babylonian exile. This section is known as the Book of Consolation, and the canticle with its beautiful imagery of God as the Shepherd is indeed consoling.

Friday of Week III (Jeremiah 14:17-21)

Jeremiah exercised his ministry during a turbulent time of faithlessness and consequent destruction. This canticle is a lament over the destruction of Jerusalem in 587 B.C. In our world we are never at a loss for situations which call us to offer this canticle in an apostolic spirit.

Saturday of Week III (Wisdom 9:1-6, 9-11)

The Book of Wisdom was compiled around 100 B.C. probably in Alexandria in Egypt to help the Jews living there to overcome the adverse influence of foreign philosophies upon their faith. Today's canticle is composed as if coming from the mouth of Solomon, a model of wisdom in Israelite tradition. Wisdom in the Bible is practical, not theoretical; it is concerned with the proper way of living, not with abstractions. Although I pray for wisdom when I come to this canticle in the breviary, I also remember to offer it especially in the person of those who bear grave responsibilities, such as the pope and the bishops, world leaders, the president and all who hold public office.

Sunday of Week IV (Daniel 3:52-57)

Please see the comments for Sunday of Week II.

Monday of Week IV (Isaiah 42:10-16)

The prophet — not Isaiah himself, but a disciple — promised the exiles in Babylon that their captivity would soon be at an end. He is so confident that this canticle anticipates deliverance and praises God for his saving power. Within the canticle God admits that for a while during the people's captivity he was inactive for his own providential reasons:

> I have looked away and kept silence,
> I have said nothing, holding myself in;
> but now I cry out as a woman in labor,
> gasping and panting.

God then declares that he will act. The image of the woman in labor is left for us to complete by realizing that in the return from exile God gives new birth to his people. This is a prayer to offer in the person of those who await the action of God and are tempted to think that God has abandoned them.

Tuesday of Week IV (Daniel 3:26, 27, 29, 34-41)

This canticle reflects the wretched condition of the people under the Greek tyrant, Antiochus IV Epiphanes, who ruled Palestine from 175-164 B.C. It is a community admission of sinfulness.

Wednesday of Week IV (Isaiah 61:10-62:5)

This canticle is from the third part of Isaiah which is a collection of prophecies in the century following the exile. It is a hymn of joyful thanksgiving.

Thursday of Week IV (Isaiah 66:10-14a)

This is another canticle from the third part of Isaiah after the exile. Jerusalem is presented as a nursing and affectionate mother, a beautiful image of the Church.

Friday of Week IV (Tobit 13:8-11, 13-15)

Please see the comments for Tuesday of Week I about the Book of Tobit. Even though after the exile Jerusalem never again enjoyed the glory of earlier times, Tobit expresses great love for Jerusalem and offers beautiful thanks and praise to God for this city, his spiritual mother.

Saturday of Week IV (Ezekiel 36:24-28)

In this canticle God speaks, promising a new covenant. We believe that God's promise is fulfilled through the covenant sealed in the blood of Christ, the blood of the new and everlasting covenant.

More canticles are found in Appendix I of the four volume set which is entitled, "Canticles and Gospel Readings for Vigils." They are so beautiful that it is a shame they could not have been incorporated into the regular four week cycle. To give a flavor of these canticles, I re-print here my favorite, which is from Isaiah 63:1-5, one of the songs of the suffering servant. We are invited to pray these songs as fulfilled in Christ:

Who is this that comes from Edom,
in crimsoned garments, from Bozrah —
this one arrayed in majesty,
marching in the greatness of his strength?

"It is I, who announce vindication,
I who am mighty to save."
Why is your apparel red,
and your garments like those of the wine presser?

"The wine press I have trodden alone,
and of my people there was no one with me.
I trod them in my anger,
and trampled them down in my wrath;
their blood spurted on my garments,
all my apparel I stained.

For the day of vengeance was in my heart,
my year for redeeming was at hand.
I looked about, but there was no one to help,
I was appalled that there was no one to lend support;
so my own arm brought about the victory
and my own wrath lent me its support."

Rich indeed is the Word of God, not only as proclaimed to us, but as prayer which is offered to the Lord our God.

CHAPTER SIXTEEN

Directives For Praying in Common

"They devoted themselves to the apostles'
teaching and the common life, to the breaking of
bread and the prayers." (Acts 2:42)

SOME OF MY JESUIT FRIENDS readily admit that their Order is not renowned for the smoothness of their liturgical ceremonies. They say that Jesuits usually consider a liturgy to have been a success when no one gets hurt.

Liturgical rules should not be hurtful but helpful. They are not meant to be absolute and unbending. Rigidity inhibits the joy which should characterize our public prayer and can turn liturgy, which should be the expression of the loving relationship between God and his children, into a chore to be endured. Precision in execution is not the object of liturgical worship; rather, the goal for which we strive is a prayerful spirit which leads us to worship God together in spirit and in truth.

The Liturgy of the Hours offers the opportunity for more creativity than does the celebration of the Holy Eucharist or the other sacraments. Some helpful options may be found among the following: significant pauses for reflection after the psalms and the reading, introductions to the psalms, especially to suggest the manner of praying them in an apostolic spirit, distributing roles which are suggested by different speakers in the original version of the psalms, a reflection after the reading by one or even several persons, changing posture or processing to express the meaning of a psalm.

On the other hand, too many variations inhibit the sense of ritual. Familiarity with how the prayer is offered is comforting and gives a sense of being at home. Participants should not have to wonder "What is coming next?" or "How long will all this last?" or even "What great new thing are we going to do today?" Liturgy learns a lesson from little children (remember Jesus said, "Unless you become like little children you cannot enter the kingdom of heaven"). Children love repetition. Try putting a little girl to bed and saying, "Tonight I am going to tell you a new story." She wants none of that. She much prefers the old, familiar story which somehow for a child is always new.

I have an image in my mind of a father playing with his small son in a swimming pool. He lifts him under his arm pits and throws him high into the air. The little boy comes down, sinks beneath the water, and then pops up, water streaming from his eyes, his nose, and his mouth. As soon as he gets his breath, he says to his Dad, "Do it again!" That is ritual, and what is true of little children at bed time or at play is valid for us at prayer.

Actually even though ritual is part of childhood, it is also a mark of spiritual maturity. Progress in prayer requires our being self-starters, people who come to prayer to be active, not passive, and who cooperate with creative elements without being dependent on them (or criticizing them). The Church fosters the externals of prayer but only to help, and not substitute for, the internal dispositions which are essential.

Having said all that, I recognize that those who pray in common often wish to know the recommended manner of offering the Liturgy of the Hours. The following directives, although taken from official sources or traditional practices, should be interpreted liberally.

Posture

All stand during the introductory verse of each hour, during the hymn, during the Gospel canticles of Zechariah, Mary, and Simeon, during the intercessions, the Lord's Prayer, and the concluding prayer. All are seated for the psalms and the canticles which are not from the Gospel, and while listening to the readings. Kneeling is not recommended during the Liturgy of the Hours.

Roles

Distributing roles manifests the nature of the Church as the body of Christ.[1] If a priest or deacon is present, he ordinarily presides.[2] Otherwise, one of the community should be chosen for this role. The presider begins the Office with the opening verse, introduces the intercessions and the Lord's Prayer, and says the concluding prayer. An ordained presider also greets, blesses, and dismisses the participants. The presider should not take the role of others.

The one who says the antiphons may also lead the response to the readings and state the intercessions. If possible, a different person should do the reading. In fact, it is desirable to divide the roles as much as possible ("Get everybody into the act").

Psalms, Canticles, and Antiphons

All should be seated before the psalms are begun. Ordinarily participants should be seated in such a way that there are two groups. This is so that they may alternate the verses of the psalms. The person who does the antiphon, known as the "antiphonarian," should read it all the way through. Those who are on the same side as the antiphonarian take up the first verse and then the two groups alternate saying the

---

[1] See the *Constitution on the Liturgy*, no. 2 and no. 28. See also 1 Corinthians 12:4.
[2] *General Instruction* of the *Liturgy of the Hours*, no. 254.

remaining verses. The antiphon may be repeated after the psalm or canticle. A community should agree on what seems better to them. Some feel that since the antiphon introduces the reading, it should not be repeated at the end. Generally in singing, however, it seems suitable to repeat the antiphon.

Psalm Prayer

The "psalm prayers" are a supplement to the psalms and are optional. They are not "official." (In the Latin edition of the breviary they are found in an appendix, but the editors of the English translation placed a prayer after each psalm for convenience.) There is no obligation to say the psalm prayers either aloud or silently. My personal preference is to allow a period of silence after each psalm, and those who wish may use that time to say the psalm prayer silently or simply to reflect on the psalm which has just been prayed.

Pauses

It is very helpful to pause for silent reflection after each psalm and non-Gospel canticle, and after the reading. A priest or deacon may give a brief homily after the Scripture reading. Other presiders may give a reflection, as may also anyone else in the community who is invited to do so.

Intercessions

There may be spontaneous intercessions added to the ones assigned to each day, but at Evening Prayer the last intercession is always the one for the dead. The phrase in italics or bold print after the introduction to the intercessions indicates the response which may be used when the person who leads the intercessions says both parts of the intercession. It is voiced only in that instance and only following the intercessions themselves.

Pacing

Due regard must be given to a deliberate and unhurried recitation of all the prayers. Rushing through the prayers inhibits piety, distracts from the meaning of the prayer, and suggests that what we are doing is not very important. Participants should listen to one another and try to stay together.

Above all we need to foster a deliberate awareness that in prayer we are privileged to fulfill the royal priesthood of the baptized, and that we pray through, with, and in Christ the Priest, united by the Holy Spirit, in the worship of our heavenly Father. Joyful, uplifting, and devout should be every occasion when we respond to the prompting of the Spirit to come together in prayer.

*"Will not God do justice to his chosen who call
out to him day and night?"*
(Luke 18:7)

CHAPTER SEVENTEEN

A Dream of Church Prayer

"Your old men shall dream dreams." (Joel 3:1)

I HAVE A RECURRING DREAM. It is not a dream I have during the night while I am sleeping. It is a dream I have during the day while I am praying. Our Blessed Mother appears on the steps of a cathedral. Before her are five children. To them she declares: "It is the will of God your Father that you join his Son in offering the prayer of the Church every day."

To the oldest child, a boy, she says: "You are called David, a name which means 'beloved.' You are Morning Prayer. You represent the psalms, prayers which are beloved by God because they are the work of the Holy Spirit. You are also like Zechariah, the priest, who was the father of John the Baptist, because your prayer reaches a climax in his canticle, which some people still call in Latin the 'Benedictus.'"

To a girl, a twin of the boy, she says, "You like me are called Mary. You represent the New Testament and your prayer reaches a climax in my own canticle, the 'Magnificat.' I love you very much, and I hope that all God's people will love you too. You are Evening Prayer." To both the boy and the girl Mary says, "You two must link arms and lead the other three children who are here with you. You must inspire them and fill them with your spirit. You must attract people to yourselves. Let them embrace you before they turn their attention to the other children."

Then she speaks to a tall boy: "You are the Office of Readings. Because you are tall you can reach up to heaven to bring the Father's Word down to earth again. You are prayerful like the others, but you are quiet and reflective. You give your time to the Word in Scripture and to the many words from good people in the Church who over the centuries have had wonderful things to say about the truth."

Then to a smaller child she says, "You are Daytime Prayer. Although you are little, you reach out to span the time between Morning and Evening Prayers. You are a good child, lovingly obedient to the Father's will." This child has a question: "But beautiful lady, who are you?" Mary replies, "I am the Mother of the Church. I show you how to pray and how to be a good disciple of my Son. I learned to pray the psalms when I was a little girl like you, and I prayed them all my life. And you know what? I still pray them in union with my Son and all the saints in heaven and on earth."

Last of all Mary turns her attention to an infant who is dozing off in the arms of the child Mary, who is Evening Prayer. She says to the baby: "You are Night Prayer because you are always falling asleep, but you are very precious to God because in your sleep you show what it means to have faith and trust in God the Father and his love for you."

Then Mary speaks to all the children: "Tell God's people about yourselves, you five children. You used to be called the breviary or the Divine Office. Now you are called the Liturgy of the Hours."

In my dream Mary then seems to grow rather sad. She casts her eyes down and says softly, "I am very disappointed that people have not listened to the teachings of my Son as they have been continued in the Church through the Vatican Council. In particular I regret that they have not heeded his wish that the Liturgy of the Hours is to be the prayer of all Catholics, and not just priests and religious. Tell people to offer the prayer of the Church."

Then holding an open prayer book in her hand and looking up toward heaven, Mary disappears from sight but not from the minds and hearts of her children.

Excerpts from the *General Instruction* and the *Constitution on the Liturgy*

"Today listen to the voice of the Lord." (Psalm 95)

R EADING THIS APPENDIX IS NOT A SUBSTITUTE for reading the *General Instruction* of the *Liturgy of the Hours*, which is found at the front of the breviary, but I judged that the heart of the doctrinal points deserves emphasis. These excerpts, I may add, are the source of many of the doctrinal components I have presented and are also a form of support for the emphasis I have thought to be suitable for certain issues, especially the priesthood of Christ and our union with him. I have also included a few of the directives. Everything that follows is a direct quotation although I have taken a few liberties when I thought the translation of the Latin document could be improved.

Doctrinal Points

"Christ is the head of renewed humanity, God's mediator who prays to the Father in the name and on behalf of all people. The heart of Christ expresses God's praise in human words of adoration, propitiation, and intercession."

"Since prayer is directed to God, it should be united with Christ, for he is the Lord of all people and the one single mediator through whom we have access to God. Christ unites the whole human family to himself so closely that there is an intimate and necessary relationship between the prayer of Christ and that of the whole human race. It is in Christ alone that human religion acquires its purpose and redemptive value. There is, however, a further relationship — a special and extremely close bond between Christ and those whom he makes members of his body, the Church."

"It is the Holy Spirit who gives unity to the praying Church. The same Spirit is in Christ, in the Church as a whole, and in each baptized person. Christian prayer is not possible without the action of the Holy Spirit who unites the entire Church and leads us through the Son to the Father."

"The Church is a community and should express in prayer its communal nature. The members of the Church can pray through Christ and in the Holy Spirit alone in their rooms with the doors closed; this prayer is necessary and it is always to be encouraged. However, community prayer has a special dignity, for Christ himself said: 'Where two or three gather in my name, I shall be there with them.'"

"The Liturgy of the Hours spreads out over the many hours of the day the praise and thanksgiving of the Eucharist, the memorial of the mysteries of salvation, and the entreaty for, and the foretaste of, heavenly glory which are present in the eucharistic mystery. It is that mystery which is the center and the culmination of the entire life of the Christian community. The Liturgy of the Hours is itself a preparation for the Eucharist, since it enkindles and nourishes those attitudes which are necessary for a beneficial eucharistic celebration: a spirit of faith, hope, love, devotion, and sacrifice."

"The Liturgy of the Hours is the prayer of the Church, and it unites Christians everywhere in heart and soul. When the Church sings God's praise in the Liturgy of the Hours, it joins in that hymn of praise which is sung through all ages in the realm of heaven. The Liturgy is a foretaste of that heavenly praise which, according to the Book of Revelation, is sung constantly before the throne of God and the Lamb."

Select Directives

Now follow a few excerpts which are in the nature of directives or ideals regarding the manner in which the Hours are celebrated:

"The testimony of the early Church indicates that the people devoted certain times to prayer. In various places it soon became the custom to set aside special times of the day for common prayer: the hour of dusk when daylight waned and the evening lamps were lighted, or the hour of dawn when the rising sun dispelled the darkness of night. As time went on, other hours too were sanctified by prayer in common."

"Whenever possible, groups of the faithful should come together in church to celebrate the principal hours of the Liturgy. The most important of these groups are the local parishes, the cells of the diocese, established under the leadership of a pastor who takes the place of the bishop. Since parishes in a certain way represent the visible Church as it is established throughout the world, they should celebrate the principal hours publicly in church whenever it is possible."

"Sacred ministers and all clerics who live together or come together on occasion, even though they are not bound to common celebration, should arrange to say at least some hours of the Liturgy in common, particularly Morning and Evening Prayer."

"Whenever groups of the laity meet for prayer, apostolic work, or some other religious reason, they are encouraged to take part in the Church's office by celebrating some of the Liturgy of the Hours. Such groups should keep in mind that it is especially in the Liturgy that one adores God the Father in spirit and in truth, and they should be aware that, particularly through liturgical worship, their common prayer has an impact on all people and contributes to the salvation of the whole world."

"It is fitting too that families in their role as domestic sanctuaries of the Church take an even greater part in the Church's life, not only offering common prayer to God, but also by celebrating some hours of the Liturgy."

"Of all the members of the Church the bishop should be first in prayer. When he prays the Liturgy of the Hours, he always does so in the name and on behalf of the Church committed to his care."

"Presbyters in union with the bishop and the whole presbyterium also represent Christ the priest in a special way. They too share the duty to pray to God on behalf of the people entrusted to them, and indeed on behalf of the whole world."

"When people pray the Liturgy of the Hours they are saying the psalms not just in their own name but truly in the name of the whole Church. They are in fact praying in the person of Christ."

"In praying the Liturgy of the Hours one is never praying privately, even when one sits alone reciting some hour of the Liturgy. Even then that person is praying the psalms of the Church's public worship and is praying in the name of the whole Church."

Excerpts from the Constitution on the Liturgy

"Christ joins the entire community of humankind to himself, associating it with his own singing of this canticle of divine praise" (83).

"Christ continues his priestly work through the agency of his Church, which is ceaselessly engaged in praising the Lord and interceding for the salvation of the whole world" (83).

"This is the prayer which Christ himself, together with his body, addresses to the Father" (84).

"Because it is the public prayer of the Church, the Divine Office is a source of piety and nourishment for personal prayer" (90).

Conclusion

When the first edition of the revised Liturgy of the Hours was promulgated on Easter Sunday, April 11, 1971, the decree of the Roman Congregation for Divine Worship stated: "From ancient times the Church has had the custom of celebrating each day the Liturgy of the Hours. In this way the Church fulfills the Lord's precept to pray without ceasing, at once offering its praise to God the Father and interceding for the salvation of the world."

Ours is a precious heritage. Through the Liturgy of the Hours we have been given a beautiful gift so that as people of faith we may come together in prayer.

> St. John's Seminary
> Camarillo, California
> Easter Sunday, April 3, 1994

"O God, be merciful to me, a sinner."
(Luke 18:13)

Summary

"By your gift I will utter praise in the vast assembly."
(Psalm 22:26)

1. Because of its emphasis on the psalms, the Liturgy of the Hours is different from ways of praying which were formative for most of us in our early impressions. As inspired prayers, the psalms are of unique value and we go to them and to the entire liturgy not to find favorite prayers but to be formed according to the movement of the Spirit.

2. A knowledge of the psalms contributes to a more prayerful attitude in their use, but such knowledge need not be esoteric. The psalms are both human and divine.

3. The poetic aspect of the psalms makes of them a memorable and aesthetically pleasing way in which to pray.

4. The "humanity" of the psalms makes them appropriate as an apostolic prayer to be offered in the person of others through our mutual union in Christ.

5. The liturgy is not intended to exhaust one's prayer life or to substitute for private prayer. In fact, private prayer is quite necessary, especially as a preparation for liturgical prayer.

6. We must continually remind ourselves to pray the psalms in an apostolic spirit, in the person of others, without excluding ourselves. Apostolic prayer is the heart of the Liturgy of the Hours.

7. In union with Christ the celebration of the Liturgy of the Hours is a joyful, communal experience of God's ever-present love for us.

8. In our first waking moments we are to look toward heaven and praise God for his goodness. The beginning of the day suggests the theme of the beginnings of salvation history, the Old Testament, but as seen in the light of the resurrection of Christ.

9. The time for Evening Prayer, when the day is at its full, sets the theme of the fullness of revelation in the New Testament. It is eminently the prayer of the Church in imitation of Mary, the type and model of the Church. Every Vespers is situated in that supper hour when Jesus, having loved his own who were in the world, showed the depth of his love.

10. The principal theme of Daytime Prayer is dedication to God's will in union with Jesus Christ who, because he was obedient unto death, was exalted by the Father.

11. The emphasis in the Office of Readings is on a meditative listening to God's word in Scripture and other sources.

12. In Night Prayer sleep is a symbol of death. The theme is complete trust and confidence: "Into your hands I commend my spirit."

13. We need not think that praying the psalms intelligently demands a profound and professional understanding, but we should try to grow constantly in our knowledge of the psalms and our dedication to them.

14. In Evening Prayer the Church has restored to liturgical use canticles which are doctrinally rich and poetically beautiful.

15. The canticles of Morning Prayer, in accord with the theme of early morning, are taken from the Old Testament.

16. Like the first Christians, we are called to come together in prayer.

17. Do we need a message from heaven to arrive at the conviction that the Liturgy of the Hours, the prayer book of the Church, is God's will for all of us so that we may come together in prayer?